Future Gen

Human Body

WHAT'S INSIDE

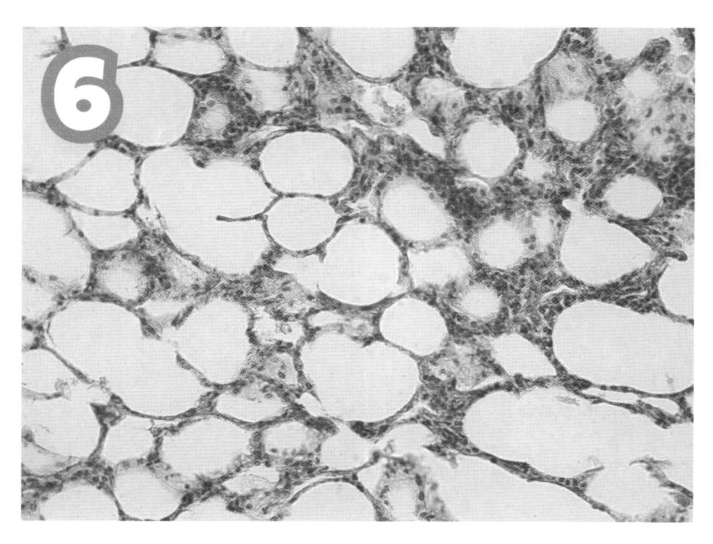

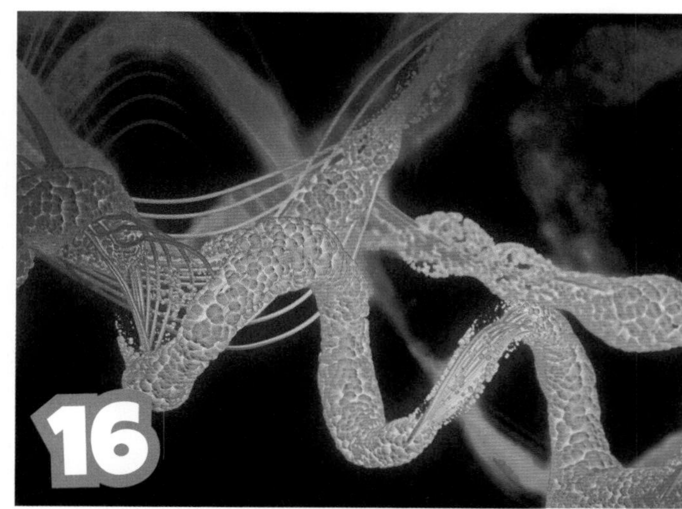

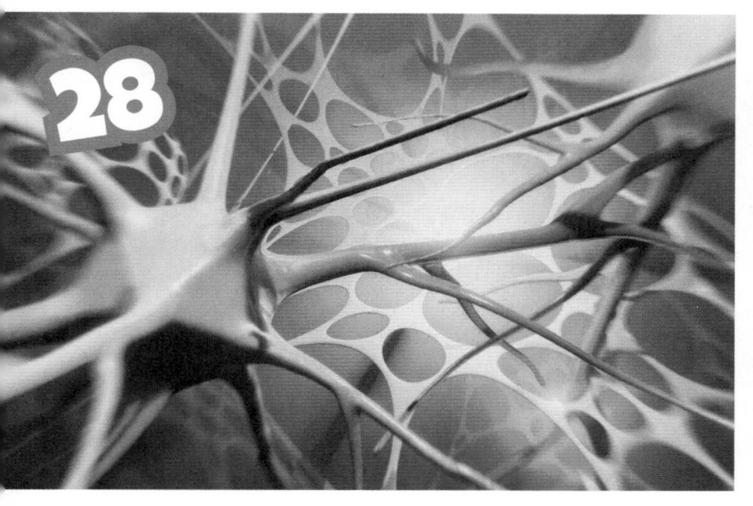

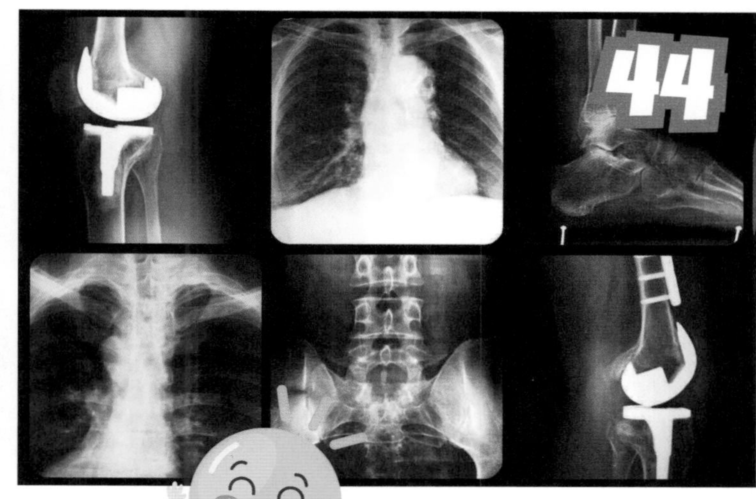

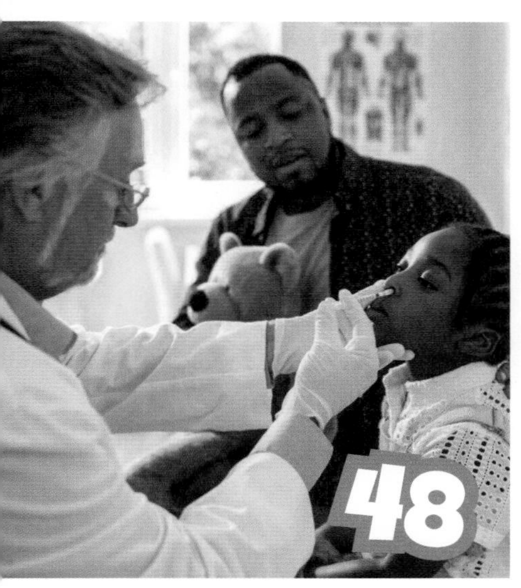

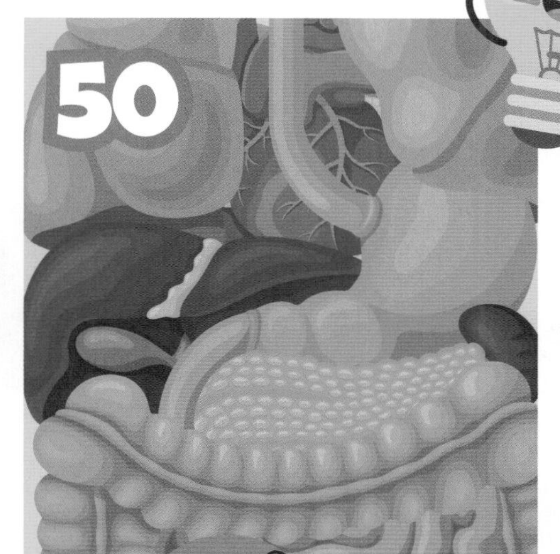

INTERACTIVE EXPERIENCE

Scan the QR code with your device's camera or download a free QR code reader app. Many iPhone and Android devices include these features

When you see the "Scan with your phone or tablet" prompt, use your device to scan the QR code, which looks like this

Hold your mobile device over the image and watch it come to life! Your device needs to be connected to the internet for this to function

MEET YOUR CELLS

Have you ever wondered what your body is made of? The answer is cells! They make up every part of your body, from your muscles and bones, to your liver and brain.

Cells work a little bit like bricks, and a little bit like factories. They build your body, and they make all the things you need to stay alive.

Most cells are much too small to see with your eyes, and they are almost completely see-through! To get a closer look at your cells, you need to use a microscope and some special pink and purple dye.

If you look at pictures of cells taken with microscopes, you will see lots of little pink blobs. They come in different shapes and sizes depending on what type of cell they are. Some like to grow in neat lines, others like to grow in stacks, and some prefer to grow all on their own.

One thing most cells have in common under the microscope is a dark purple dot at their center. That dot is one of the most important parts of the cell; you will find out more about it a bit later.

If you looked at pictures of all the cells in your body, you would probably notice something else too; some of them aren't human!

Many of the cells in your body are actually bacteria! That might sound scary, but not all bacteria make you sick. The ones inside you right now are helping you to stay healthy. Most of them live in your intestines, where they help you to get all the energy and goodness out of your food. Without them you would feel very hungry indeed.

Over the next few pages, you will learn more about the cells in your body, what's inside them, what they do, and how they help you grow!

HOW MANY CELLS DO YOU HAVE?

There are an enormous amount of cells in your body – about 37 trillion to be exact. That's a really big number!

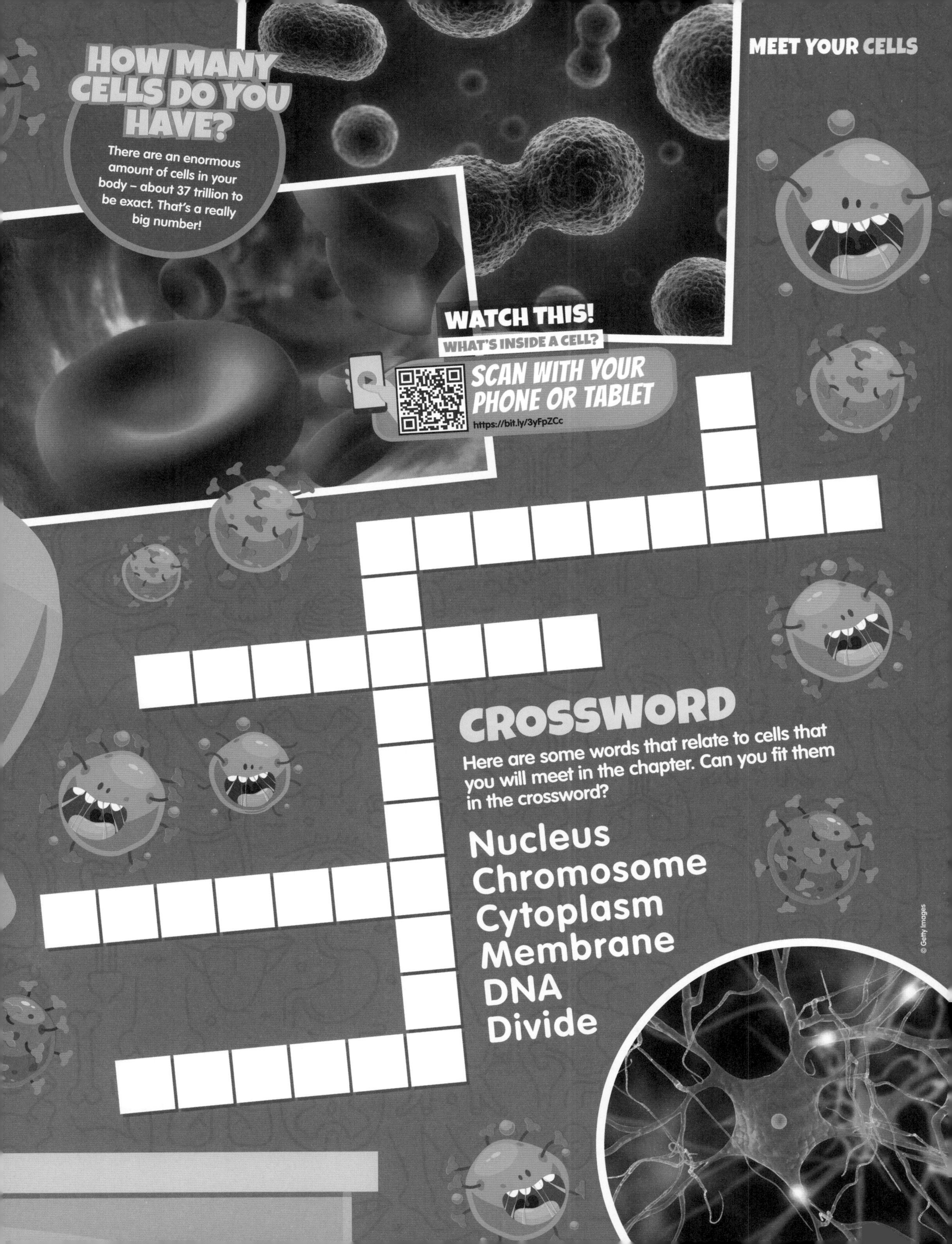

CROSSWORD

Here are some words that relate to cells that you will meet in the chapter. Can you fit them in the crossword?

Nucleus
Chromosome
Cytoplasm
Membrane
DNA
Divide

© Getty Images

THE CELL: WHAT YOUR BODY'S MADE OF

You are made of cells – trillions of them! They are the living bricks that make up the human body. There are more than 200 different types, and each one has its own special job to do. There are cells that make sweat in your armpits, cells that make tears in your eyes, and cells that make wax in your ears!

Your brain and nervous system are made of nerve cells, which work like tiny telephone wires; they send messages from one part of your body to another. Some nerve cells stretch from your backbone right down to your toes! Just imagine how long they'll be when you're fully grown.

Your arms and legs are made of skin cells, fat cells, muscle cells, and bone cells. They protect you from the outside world, store energy, move your body, and keep your skeleton strong.

Your digestive system is a mix of gland cells, lining cells, and muscle cells. The gland cells make the digestive juices that break your food down into nutrients. The lining cells take all those nutrients in, and the muscle cells keep everything moving, from your mouth right down to your bottom.

Even your blood is made of cells! There are red blood cells that carry oxygen around your body, and there are white blood cells that fight bacteria or viruses that try to make you sick.

Most cells decide what job they are going to do before you are even born, but some wait to choose until later. Scientists call these cells "stem cells." They can turn into almost any other cell in the body! They help you to heal when you get hurt, and replace your old cells when they wear out.

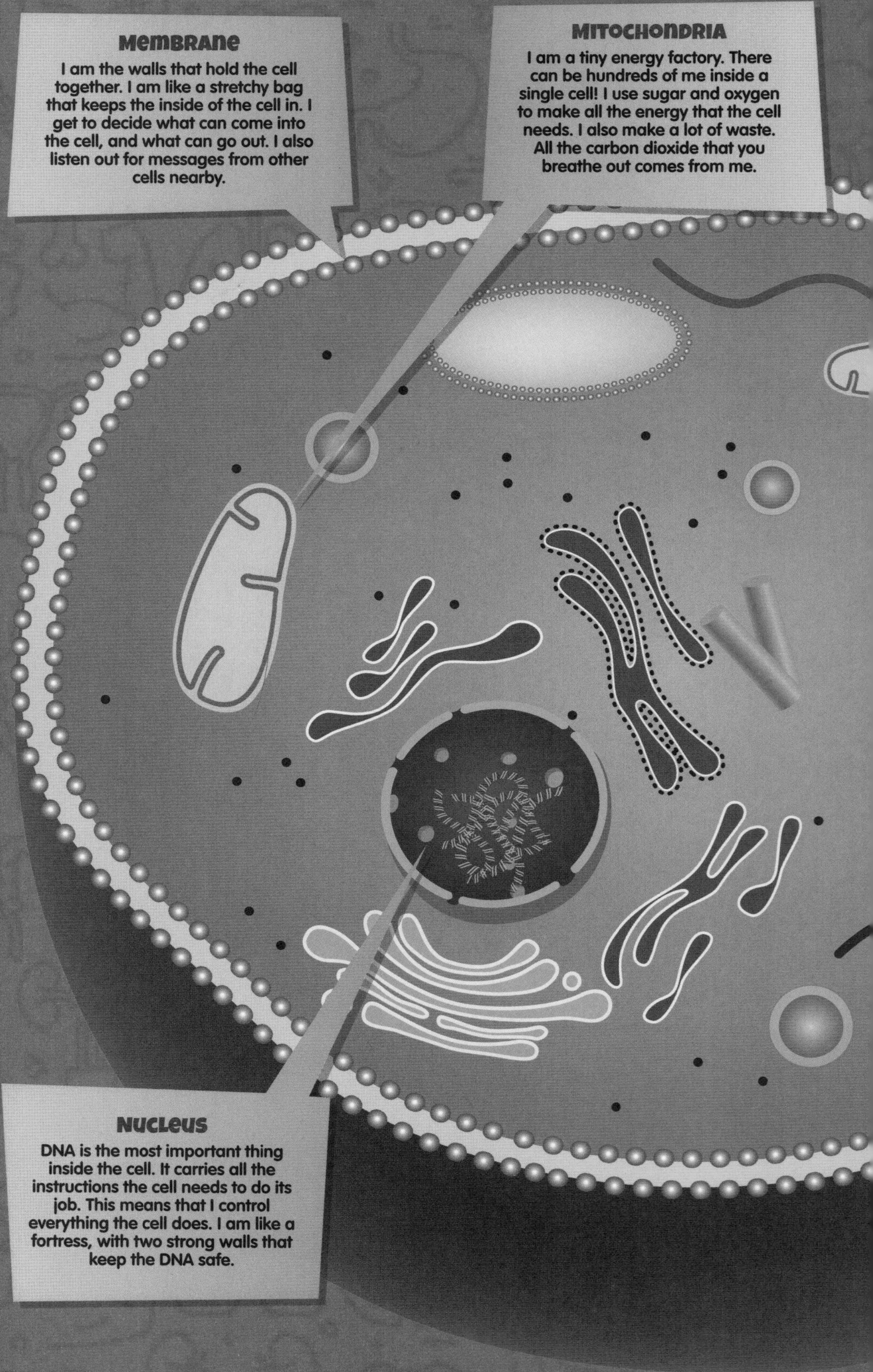

Membrane

I am the walls that hold the cell together. I am like a stretchy bag that keeps the inside of the cell in. I get to decide what can come into the cell, and what can go out. I also listen out for messages from other cells nearby.

Mitochondria

I am a tiny energy factory. There can be hundreds of me inside a single cell! I use sugar and oxygen to make all the energy that the cell needs. I also make a lot of waste. All the carbon dioxide that you breathe out comes from me.

Nucleus

DNA is the most important thing inside the cell. It carries all the instructions the cell needs to do its job. This means that I control everything the cell does. I am like a fortress, with two strong walls that keep the DNA safe.

TEST YOURSELF 3

Memorize the facts, close the book, and write them down. How many can you remember and jot down in three minutes?

FIVE THINGS YOU NEED TO KNOW ABOUT CELLS

How many of these facts surprise you and your friends?

HEART CELLS BEAT ON THEIR OWN

The cells in your heart can beat by themselves without any instructions from your brain.

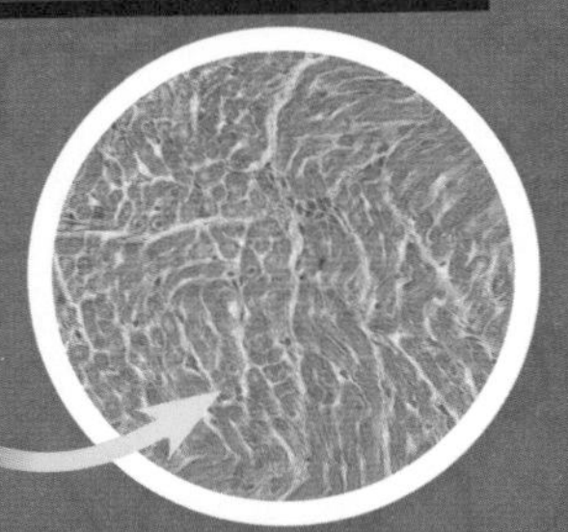

LIVER CELLS CLEAN YOUR BLOOD

The cells in your liver take chemicals out of your blood and break them down.

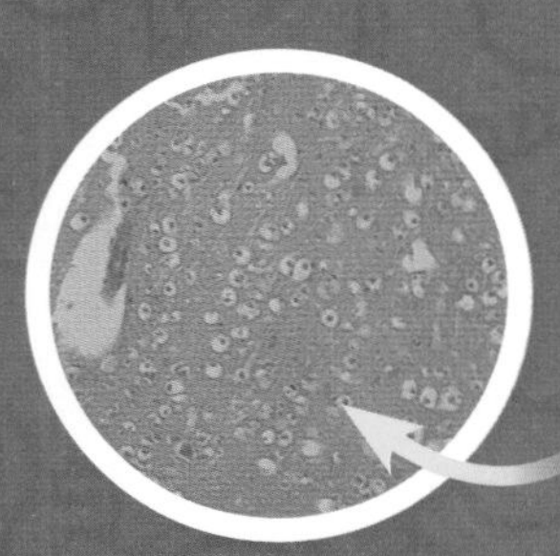

BRAIN CELLS MAKE ELECTRICITY

The cells in your brain are like living wires; they make electric currents.

STOMACH CELLS MAKE ACID

The cells in your stomach make acid more sour than lemon juice.

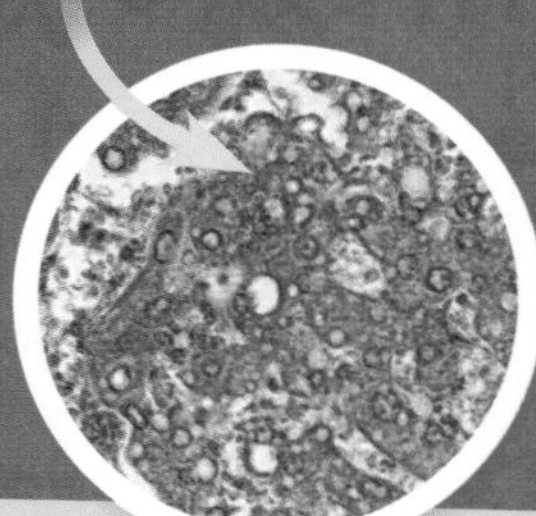

LUNG CELLS LET AIR THROUGH

The cells in your lungs are so thin that air can cross through them into your blood.

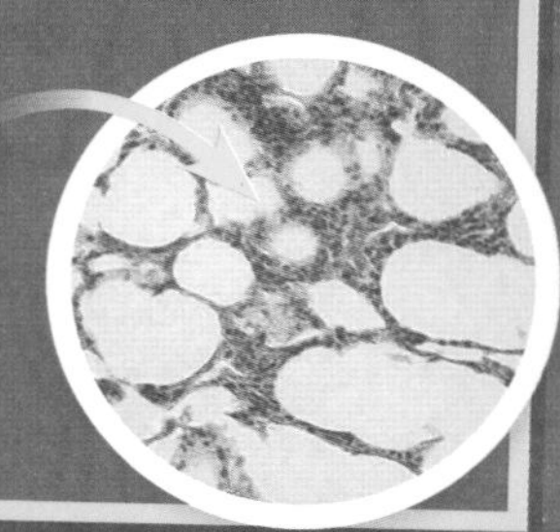

TRY IT OUT!

Discover DNA at home!

WHAT YOU'LL NEED

- A plastic bag
- A strawberry
- Two teaspoons of liquid soap
- One teaspoon of salt
- Three ounces water
- Damp coffee filter
- One-and-a-half teaspoons cold rubbing alcohol
- Two cups
- A spoon

INSTRUCTIONS

1. Put a strawberry in a plastic bag and squash it up.
2. Mix the liquid soap, salt, and water in a cup.
3. Add two teaspoons of the mixture to your plastic bag.
4. Give it another good squash.
5. Put the coffee filter in the other cup.
6. Pour the strawberry mixture through the filter.
7. Take the filter out of the cup.
8. Pour the alcohol gently on top of the strawberries.
9. Look inside – do you see white strands?
10. Scoop them out with your spoon. That's DNA!

WHAT HAVE YOU LEARNED?

You've just pulled the DNA out of a strawberry! The liquid soap broke the strawberry cells open, the salt released their DNA, and the alcohol made the DNA stick together so that you could see it. Don't worry if it didn't work the first time – science is like that sometimes. Give it another try!

CYTOPLASM

Cells run on chemical reactions. It's my job to make sure they happen in the right place and at the right time. I am mostly water, and everything inside the cell floats in me. I also have a kind of skeleton that helps the cell keep its shape.

© Getty Images

HOW YOUR CELLS GO THROUGH CYCLES

Your body started out as one cell. Just one! That one cell became two cells. Those two cells became four cells. Those four cells became eight cells. And they kept doubling and doubling until there were enough cells to make all of you. One day, when you're finished growing, you will have more than 100 trillion cells inside your body. That means your cells will have doubled more than ten million times!

So how does one cell turn into 100 trillion cells? The answer is the cell cycle. This is the name scientists give to the way that a cell divides, or splits in two. Scientists call it a cell cycle because cells can divide more than once. They go through all the steps in a loop, getting ready to divide, dividing, and then growing, before getting ready to divide again.

Before a cell divides, it needs to make sure that the new cell will have its own copy of the DNA. Without genes, the new cell wouldn't know what to do, so the cell copies its DNA and sorts one copy to one side and one copy to the other.

This sorting step can be tricky. DNA is long and stringy, so if the cell tried to pull it apart, it would get in a knot! It solves this problem by packing the DNA down into little X-shaped packages called chromosomes. It attaches a string to each of these packages and pulls them to where they need to be.

When everything is in place, the cell is finally ready to split in two. To do this, it pinches itself together in the middle, and pops in half like a soap bubble.

WORD JIGSAW

Fit the jigsaw pieces together to create some words related to your cells.

ODD ONE OUT

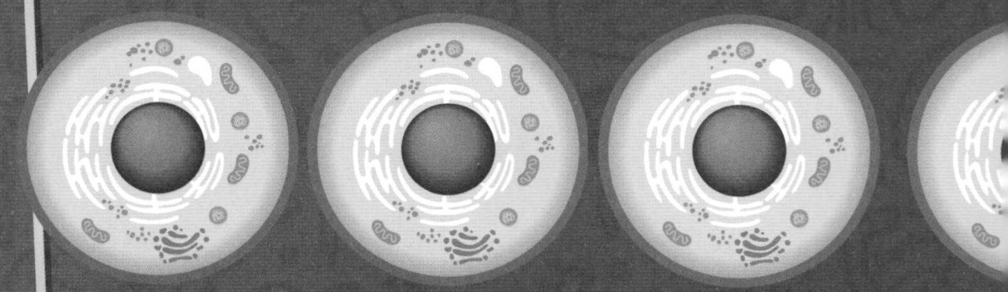

FIND THE CELL THAT IS UNIQU

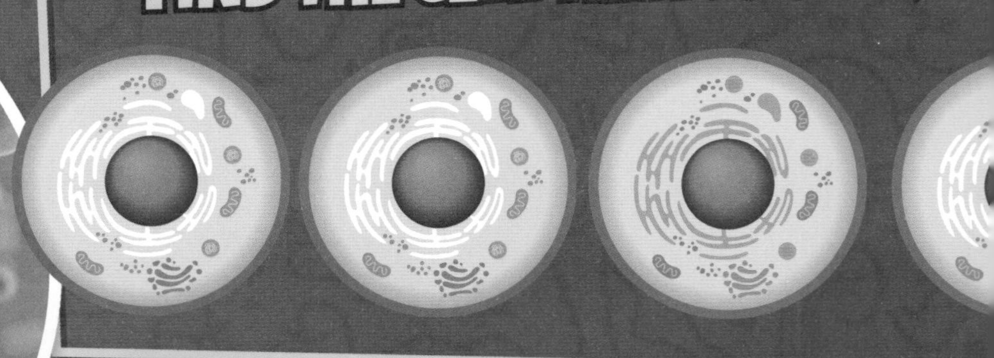

GROW AND WORK

The cell spends most of its time growing and doing its normal job in the body.

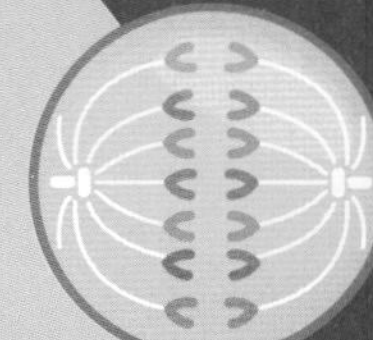

MAKE DNA

When it's time to divide, the cell copies all of its DNA.

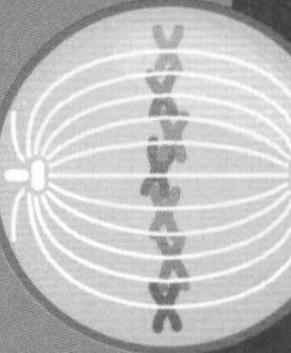

GROW SOME MORE

The cell grows bigger so that it will be big enough to split in half.

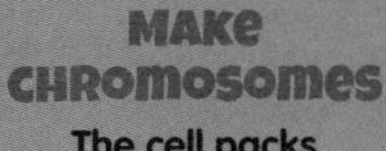

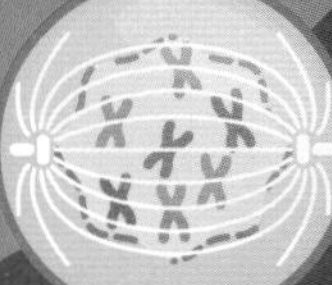

MAKE CHROMOSOMES

The cell packs its DNA into X-shapes called chromosomes.

FREE THE DNA

The nucleus breaks open and tiny strings grab hold of the chromosomes.

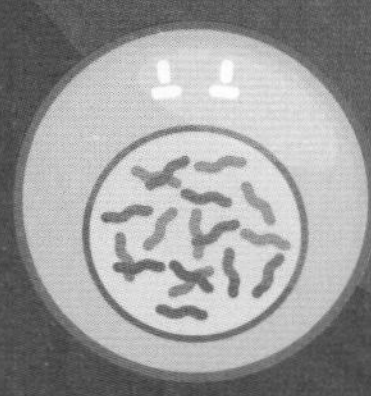

LINE THE CHROMOSOMES UP

The cell pulls the chromosomes into a line across its middle.

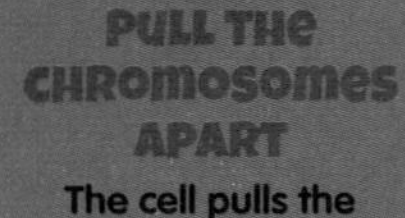

PULL THE CHROMOSOMES APART

The cell pulls the chromosomes apart, taking one set to each side.

SPLIT IN TWO

The cell builds a new nucleus around each set of chromosomes.

DAUGHTER CELLS

The cell splits into two new "daughter cells." They're like identical twins.

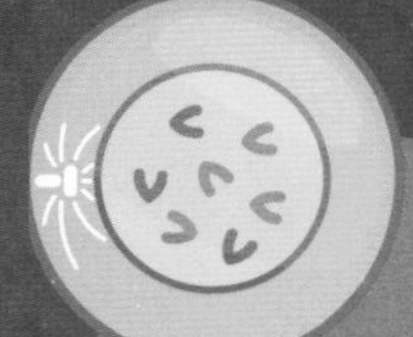

REST

Some cells stop dividing and take a rest from the cell cycle.

BIG NUMBERS

100 TRILLION
THERE ARE ONE HUNDRED TRILLION CELLS INSIDE YOUR BODY

69 MILLION
YOU MAKE SIXTY NINE MILLION NEW CELLS EVERY SINGLE MINUTE

100 BILLION
NEWBORN BABIES ALREADY HAVE 100 BILLION BRAIN CELLS

200 BILLION
YOU MAKE 200 BILLION NEW RED BLOOD CELLS EVERY DAY

© Getty Images

NUCLEUS: YOUR CELLS" BRAIN

Remember at the beginning of the chapter when you learned that cells have a really important purple dot right in the center? That dot is the nucleus. It's the brain of the cell!

The nucleus contains your DNA, which works a bit like an instruction manual. It carries your genes, which have all the information that your cells need to build and look after your body.

Your DNA is six-and-a-half feet long, and has just over 20,000 genes. That's a lot of instructions!

You might be wondering how almost seven whole feet of DNA can possibly fit inside a tiny nucleus! Amazing, isn't it? To fit it all in, the cell winds it around special beads called histones (pronounced hiss-tones), a bit like winding sewing thread around a spool.

The nucleus controls the cell by printing off different parts of the genetic instructions from your DNA. It copies them into a type of code called RNA. It then sends that code out into the cell through tiny holes in its membrane.

In the cytoplasm of the cell, machines called ribosomes pick up the RNA and use the instructions to make more machines called proteins. These proteins change what the cell is doing. Some make it grow, some make it divide, and some make it do special jobs, like making hormones.

The nucleus is one of the most important parts of a cell. But some cells don't have one! Can you guess which?

It's your red blood cells! They are so busy carrying oxygen that they don't have space for a nucleus. This means that they don't know how to fix themselves when they break. Your body has to make new red blood cells all the time to replace the ones that wear out.

MAKE A LIST!

Name some things that have a nucleus and write them down in the spaces below.

HUMAN BODY CELLS

LIVER

Liver cells have a small round nucleus right in the very middle.

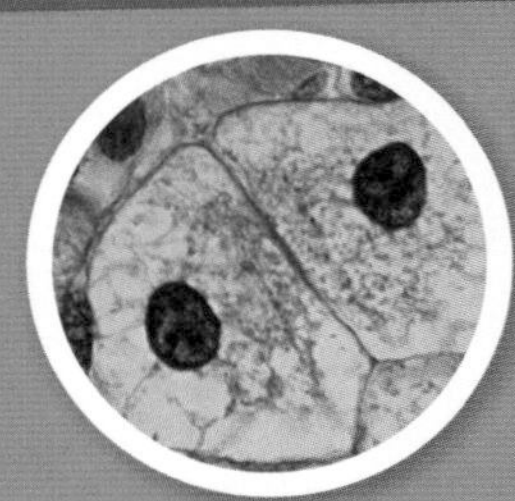

BLOOD

The nucleus of a white blood cell is not always round. Some have three parts!

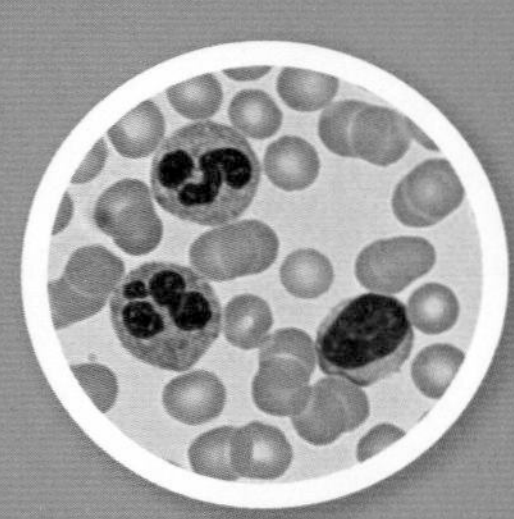

FAT

The nucleus of a fat cell gets squashed right to the edge.

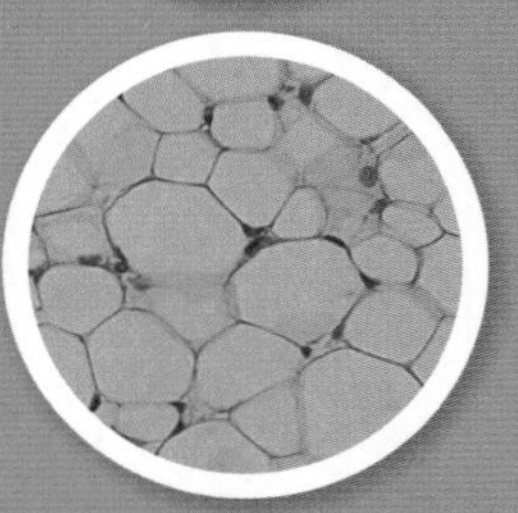

MUSCLE

Muscle cells have more than one nucleus! Look at all the dark spots in this picture.

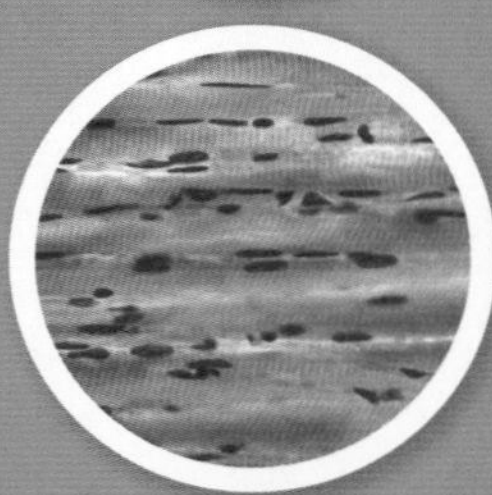

HOW DO I PRONOUNCE NUCLEUS?

This word has three syllables. You say it like this:
new-klee-us

QUIZ

HOW MUCH DO YOU KNOW ABOUT THE NUCLEUS?

WHAT IS INSIDE THE NUCLEUS?

A: Blood
B: DNA
C: Fat

WHERE CAN YOU FIND THE NUCLEUS?

A: In the middle of the cell
B: Outside the cell
C: In the brain

WHAT DOES THE NUCLEUS DO?

A: Digests food
B: Controls the cell
C: Makes energy

WHAT KIND OF CELL HAS MORE THAN ONE NUCLEUS?

A: Skin cell
B: Red blood cell
C: Muscle cell

WHAT KIND OF CELL HAS NO NUCLEUS?

A: Skin cell
B: Red blood cell
C: Muscle cell

HOW LONG IS THE DNA INSIDE A NUCLEUS?

A: Seven centimeters
B: Six inches
C: Six-and-a-half feet

ANSWERS: B, A, B, C, B, C

WATCH THIS!

HOW IMPORTANT IS THE NUCLEUS?

SCAN WITH YOUR PHONE OR TABLET
https://bit.ly/2VxQSsK

ODD ONE OUT

A cell usually only has one nucleus. Which is the odd object out?

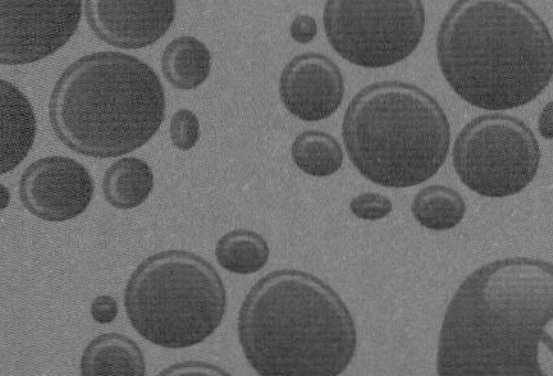
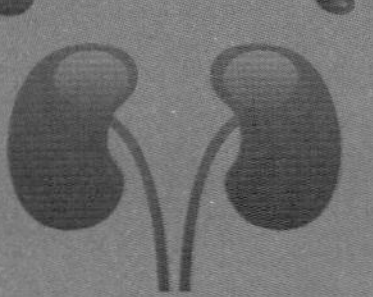
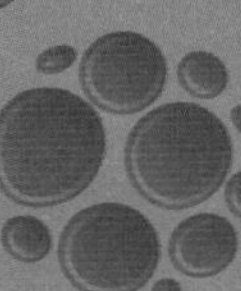
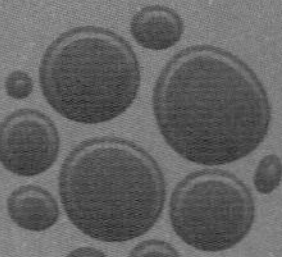
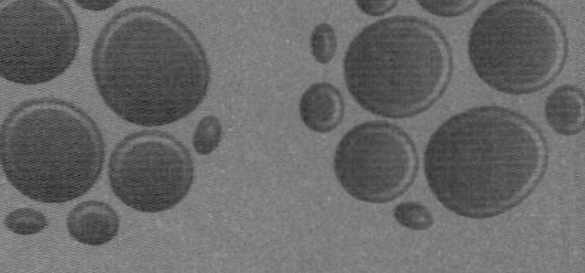
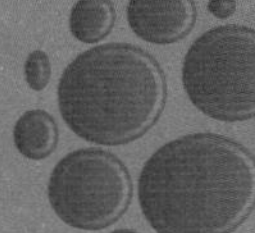

© Getty Images

RIBOSOMES: PARTICLES THAT MAKE PROTEINS

MITOCHONDRIA

QUIZ

HOW MUCH DO YOU KNOW ABOUT RIBOSOMES?

WHAT DO RIBOSOMES MAKE?

A: Juice
B: Protein
C: Energy

HOW MANY RIBOSOMES DOES A CELL HAVE?

A: Ten million
B: Ten
C: None

WHAT DO RIBOSOMES LOOK LIKE?

A: Hamburger buns
B: Kidney beans
C: Smiley faces

WHO TELLS A RIBOSOME WHAT TO DO?

A: The ear
B: The brain
C: The nucleus

HOW LONG ARE THE CODE WORDS A RIBOSOME READS?

A: 300 letters
B: Three letters
C: Three million letters

WHAT DO RIBOSOMES STICK TOGETHER?

A: Jellybeans
B: Plastic beads
C: Amino acids

ANSWERS: B, A, A, C, B, C

Ribosomes are protein factories! It's their job to make the molecular machines that keep your cells running. They look a bit like burger buns, with two parts that fit together, one on top of the other.

If you have looked at the page about proteins in this book, you'll know that proteins are made from strings of amino acids. The ribosome's job is to make those strings. They do this by sticking amino acids together in the right order, following instructions made by the cell's nucleus.

The nucleus writes the instructions for making proteins in a secret chemical code! That code is called RNA, and it has four letters: A, C, G, and U.

Ribosomes used to be the only things in the universe that could read the code. But in the 1960s, scientists cracked it too! They found out that the RNA letters spell out sixty-four different three-letter words. Each of those words means something to a ribosome.

The most important word is AUG. It means "start." It tells a ribosome to start making a new protein.

There are three words, UAG, UAA, and UGA, that mean "stop." They tell the ribosome that the protein is finished.

The other sixty words tell the ribosome what amino acid to add to the protein next.

But wait! You might remember that there are only twenty amino acids in the body. So why are there sixty words for amino acids in the code? Simple: there is more than one word for each amino acid.

Ribosomes read these code words really fast. They can stick 200 amino acids together every minute! And there are ten million ribosomes inside each of your cells. That's some serious protein-making power.

TRUE OR FALSE?

Write next to the statements whether the information about ribosomes is true or false.

RIBOSOMES ARE BIGGER THAN CELLS

RIBOSOMES CAN READ SECRET CODE

RIBOSOMES NEVER GET TIRED

ANSWERS: FALSE, TRUE, TRUE

LARGE SUBUNIT

MRNA

SMALL SUBUNIT

WATCH THIS!

HOW RIBOSOMES REALLY WORK!

The Amoeba Sisters tell you everything you need to know about your ribosomes.
https://bit.ly/3xAoYJY

WATCH A CELL MAKE INSTRUCTIONS

The Walter and Eliza Hall Institute show you how cells make instructions for ribosomes.
https://bit.ly/2X2eo1Q

TAKE A TOUR

Dr. Binocs takes you on a tour of the inside of a cell.
https://bit.ly/3s2OC9a

DISCOVER THE PRODUCTION LINE

STEM Kids show you how the protein production line works.
https://bit.ly/3yBcq6u

© Getty Images

SCAN WITH YOUR PHONE OR TABLET

MITOCHONDRIA: MAKING ENERGY

Mitochondria are tiny power plants inside your cells! They mix your food with the air you breathe to make the energy that keeps your body going.

They work a bit like power stations, but instead of burning gas to make electricity, they burn sugar to charge chemical batteries. Scientists call these batteries ATP, which stands for adenosine triphosphate (pronounced ah-den-oh-seen try-fos-fate).

To use the energy in an ATP battery, cells have to snap a piece of it off! To charge the battery, the mitochondria have to stick it back together again. This takes lots of energy.

Mitochondria get the energy they need by burning sugar and oxygen. This powers tiny pumps, which move particles called ions from one place to another.

The ions then have to get back to where they came from, and the only way to do that is through a special gate. That gate traps their energy and uses it to fix and charge the batteries.

Mitochondria have a big job to do, but they are tiny! They are just 0.001 millimeters long – 100 times smaller than a cell. They're also completely see-through, making them really tricky to spot with a normal microscope. So to see what they look like, scientists have to use big, powerful electron microscopes.

The pictures these microscopes take show that mitochondria are the same shape as kidney beans! Inside, they have lots of little folds that scientists call cristae (pronounced kris-tee). Those folds are where the energy pumps live.

Electron microscope pictures also show that different cells have different amounts of mitochondria. Some cells, like fat cells, don't use much energy, so they only have a couple. But other cells, like the ones in your heart and liver, are so busy that they have thousands!

WHAT IS OXYGEN?

Oxygen is a gas in the air. You are breathing it in right now!

WHAT IS A CARB?

A carbohydrate is a long molecule made of lots of sugar molecules stuck together.

MY OTHER JOBS

I GROW AND DIVIDE ON MY OWN!

I have my own DNA and my own genes. When my cell needs more energy, I grow and divide in order to make even more mitochondria.

I HELP CELLS TALK

Cells use chemical messages to keep track of what's going on inside them. I help to pass these messages around.

I PROTECT YOUR BODY FROM SICK CELLS!

When a cell gets sick, it can hurt your whole body. If my cell is sick, I help to get rid of it to make sure that you stay healthy.

CRISTAE

The inner membrane has lots and lots of folds. This lets it pack thousands of pumps into a tiny space. More folds mean more energy.

INNER MEMBRANE

The inner membrane has proteins that work like pumps. They pump ions out and then let them rush back again. This recharges the cell's batteries.

OUTER MEMBRANE

Mitochondria have two membranes. The outer membrane has big protein doors that let molecules like oxygen, carbon dioxide, and sugar pass through.

MATRIX

Microscopic machines called enzymes work here to release the energy from sugar and oxygen. This powers the pumps in the inner membrane.

NAME THE CARBOHYDRATES!

Mitochondria take food molecules and combine them with oxygen to make energy. Their favorite foods are carbohydrates. Can you name the carbohydrates below?

© Getty Images

ANSWERS: Bread, pasta, honey, oatmeal oats, rice, & sugar

PROTEINS & AMINO ACIDS: YOUR MICROSCOPIC MACHINES

Proteins are the molecules that do all the work inside your body. They are like microscopic machines! Your cells can make between 80,000 and 400,000 different types of protein, and they all have their own special jobs to do.

There are proteins that read DNA, proteins that punch holes in bacteria, and proteins that stop you bleeding. There are proteins that work like doors, proteins that work like trains, and proteins that work like elastic bands!

If you looked closely at any of these proteins, you would see that they are all made from long strings wrapped up into 3D shapes. If you unwrapped those strings and had an even closer look, you would notice that they are made of lots of tiny molecules. Those molecules are called amino acids.

There are twenty types of amino acids in the body. Each one has a long name, a three-letter code name, and a one-letter code name. Scientists like names!

The smallest amino acid is called glycine (pronounced gliy-seen). Its three-letter name is gly and its one-letter name is G. The biggest amino acid is called tryptophan (pronounced trip-toe-fan). Its three-letter name is trp, and its one-letter name is W.

Each amino acid is a little bit different. Some prefer to be in the middle of a protein, and others would rather be on the outside. Some like water, and others prefer oil. Some stick to other molecules, and others don't. It's the combination of these different chemical personalities that makes your proteins work the way they do.

To make a protein, all a cell needs to do is put a string of amino acids together in the right order, and fold the string up. The instructions for how to do this come from your genes. If you want to find out more about how your cells use instructions to make proteins, turn to the page about ribosomes!

WHERE CAN I FIND PROTEINS IN MY BODY?

INSIDE EVERY SINGLE CELL!

DIGESTIVE SYSTEM

BLOOD

SALIVA

SWEAT

MUCUS

DNA

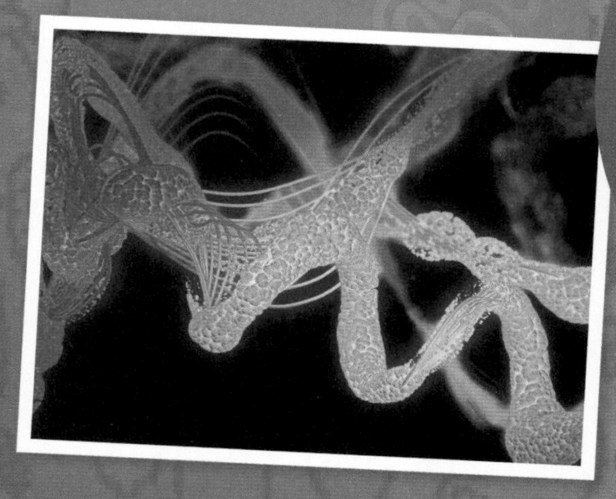

SOLVE THE SUM

Proteins make up about 20% of our bodies. Fill out the sum to make 20%.

☐ /10 x ☐ = 20%

FIVE THINGS YOU NEED TO KNOW ABOUT AMINO ACIDS

1 THERE ARE 500 AMINO ACIDS

There are hundreds of amino acids in nature, but your body only uses twenty of them.

2 AMINO ACIDS COME FROM FOOD

You can get amino acids by eating proteins made by plants and animals.

3 YOUR AMINO ACIDS ARE LEFT HANDED

Amino acids can be left or right handed. Your body almost always uses left.

4 YOU DON'T STORE AMINO ACIDS

Your body saves fat for the future, but it doesn't keep spare amino acids.

5 YOUR BODY CAN'T MAKE EVERY AMINO ACID

You can only make eleven of the amino acids, so you have to get the rest from your food.

MAKING PROTEINS

The next step is known as translation. This is when the RNA is converted into amino acids that make up the protein.

AMINO ACIDS

POLYPEPTIDE CHAINS

PROTEIN MOLECULE

COPY THE DNA

One of the major steps in making a protein is called transcription. This is where a cell makes a copy of the DNA. Help begin making a protein by copying the image in the space next to it. We call the copy RNA.

© Getty Images

ENZYMES: SPEEDING UP REACTIONS

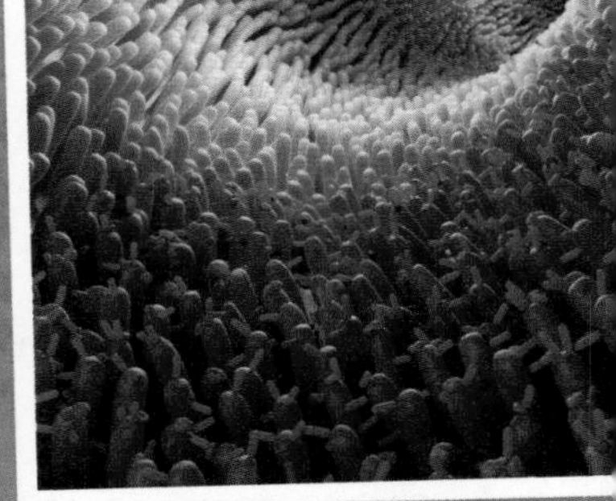

Your body is like a giant chemistry set! You are completely full of molecules that have to mix together and react to keep you alive. The trouble is that most chemical reactions happen really slowly, and your body needs them to happen fast.

Imagine if you had to wait for your dinner to break down on its own before you could get all the energy out. You'd be so hungry.

That's where enzymes come in. They make chemical reactions happen faster. Some break molecules apart, and others fix molecules together.

If you looked at an enzyme under a really powerful microscope, you would see a 3D shape with holes in its surface. Those holes grab hold of different molecules and make them react.

There are lots of different enzymes in your body, but the ones you hear about most often are the ones in your digestive system. It's their job to get the nutrients out of your food as fast as possible.

The first enzyme in your digestive system is called amylase (pronounced am-ill-ayz), which you can find in your spit. Its job is to break molecules called carbohydrates into smaller pieces called sugars. Carbohydrates you might recognize include pasta, bread, and cereal.

Have you ever noticed that these foods get sweeter as you chew them? That's because amylase is breaking them down and letting all their sugar molecules out!

Your food also contains proteins (like meat, eggs, and beans) and fats (like butter and oil). Your digestive system makes enzymes to break those down too.

Enzymes called proteases (pronounced pro-tee-aze) snap proteins into pieces called amino acids. Enzymes called lipases (pronounced lip-aze) break fats into small pieces called fatty acids.

You might have noticed that all the enzyme words end with the letters "ase." If you see other science words with those letters at the end, the chances are that they are enzymes too!

ENZYMES ARE LIKE LOCKS

It can help to imagine that an enzyme is a bit like a lock. It has a keyhole for the molecule to fit inside.

WORD SUDOKU

Played just like regular sudoku, but with letters! Remember, you can only use E, N, Z, Y, M and E. Each of the six rows and columns, as well as each of the six subregions, must contain one, and only one, of each of the six letters.

		M			
		E			Y
N			E		
	E				E
		N			
			E		M

ENZYMES DO TWO MAIN JOBS

Some enzymes break molecules apart, and other enzymes join molecules together. Both types work like locks and keys.

MAGIC SQUARES

Can you solve the magic squares? Remember, you can only use numbers from zero to nine once, and their sum of each of the rows, columns, and diagonal must equal the same.

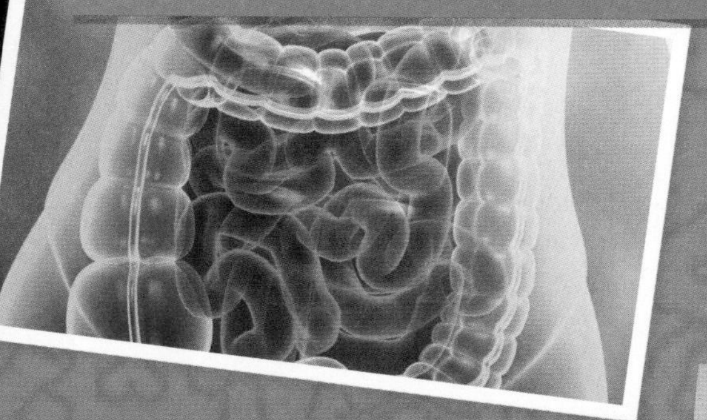

	7	6
9	5	

THE SUM IS 15

	8	1
2		6

THE SUM IS 12

Molecules are like keys

The molecule has to fit perfectly inside the enzyme keyhole for the chemical reaction to happen.

Some enzymes break molecules apart

When the enzyme (the lock) meets the right molecule (the key), they fit together, and the molecule breaks open.

Two molecules can fit in one lock

If an enzyme is joining two molecules together, both molecules have to fit into the lock at the same time.

Some enzymes join molecules together

When the two molecules meet inside the enzyme, they join together, forming one new molecule.

WHAT HAPPENS WHEN...

The pH is changed

Enzymes are sensitive to acid. If there is too much or too little, it can change their shape, stopping them from doing their job.

The concentration is changed

If you give an enzyme more work to do, it will work faster, but there is a limit. At some point it will be working as fast as it possibly can.

The temperature is changed

If the temperature goes up a little bit, enzymes work faster. But if it goes up too much, they can bend out of shape and never bend back.

We're inhibited!

Sometimes, an evil twin stops an enzyme from doing its job. It looks just like the molecule the enzyme normally works with, but it gets in the way and slows everything down!

© Getty Images

END OF CELLS

How amazing are your cells? They are so tiny, but do so much.

Each one has its own copy of the DNA instruction manual for your body. Cells use those instructions to do everything, from sending messages in your brain to digesting dinner molecules in your stomach. They fix themselves when they get broken, and replace themselves when they get old.

All the parts of the cell, like the nucleus, the ribosomes, and the mitochondria, work together to keep everything running smoothly. And all the cells in your body work together to keep you alive.

Your cells are always busy. The cells in your cheeks make a liter of spit every day. The cells on your head make a centimeter of hair every month. And while you're still growing, the cells in your bones make you two inches taller every year!

To do all these things, your body has to make billions of new cells every day, and those cells each have to make thousands of new proteins.

Most of this happens without you even realizing. In the time it took you to read this page, your body will have made 30,000 new skin cells. You didn't even notice, did you?

WATCH THIS!

LEARN MORE ABOUT YOUR CELLS

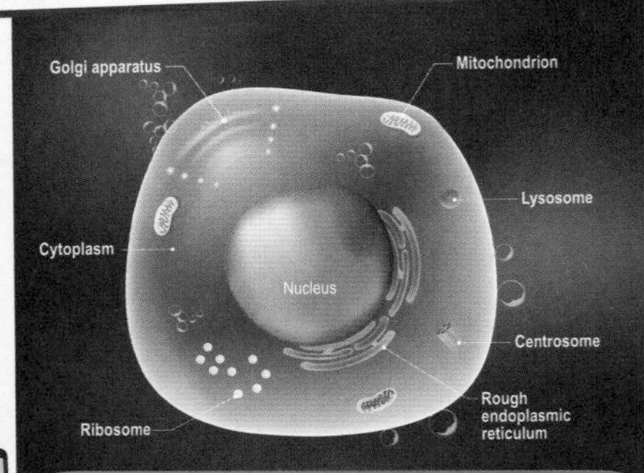

SCAN WITH YOUR PHONE OR TABLET

https://bit.ly/3lu5BQB

TEST YOURSELF! 5

Memorize the facts from this chapter, close the book, and write them down. How many can you remember and jot down in five minutes?

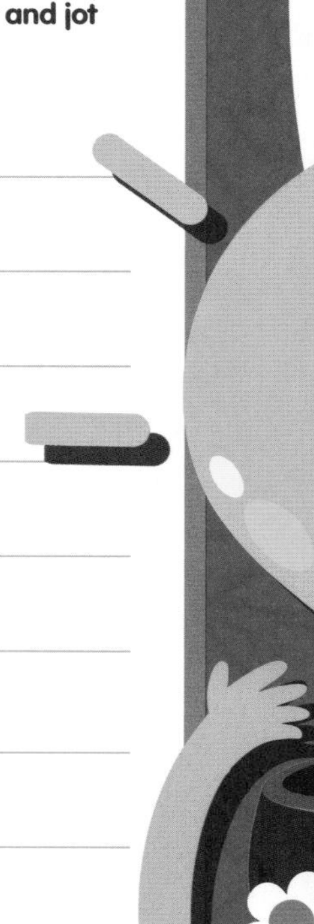

COMPLETE THE SENTENCES

Fill in the blanks with the supplied words to complete the ten sentences

1. Cells go through _______ to _______ and _______.
2. You have _______ trillion cells in your body. You make _______ million new cells each minute.
3. Before a _______ can divide. It has to _______ all of its _______.
4. The _______ is the liquid part of the cell. It is surrounded by a bag called a _______ .
5. _______ make energy from _______ and _______.
6. Ribosomes are _______ factories. They follow instructions from the _______.
7. The genetic code has _______ letters. They spell out sixty-four different _______-letter words.
8. Scientists use _______ and purple _______ to look at cells under the _______.
9. Cells get their energy from chemical _____ called _____ molecules. _____ recharge those batteries.
10. Proteins are like microscopic _____. They are made from _____ _____.

SIXTY-NINE

MITOCHONDRIA | PINK | OXYGEN

PROTEIN | NUCLEUS | CYCLES | DYE

GROW | THREE | AMINO | SUGAR

MACHINES | MICROSCOPE | CELL

RIBOSOMES | ATP | MEMBRANE

COPY | CYTOPLASM | 100 | DIVIDE

BATTERIES | FOUR | DNA | ACIDS

WATCH THIS!

DISCOVER MORE ABOUT CELL STUCTURE

SCAN WITH YOUR PHONE OR TABLET

https://bit.ly/2VxQSsK

ANSWERS: 1: Cycle, grow, divide. 2: 100, sixty-nine. 3: Cell, copy, DNA. 4: Cytoplasm, membrane 5: Mitochondria, sugar, oxygen. 6: Protein, nucleus. 7: Four, three. 8: Pink, dye, microscope. 9: Batteries, ATP, ribosomes. 10: Machines, amino, acids.

© Getty Images

CELL PUZZLES

How quickly can you work out these puzzles?

HOW MANY CELLS?

It's said that there are thirty trillion cells in the human body. How many zeros can you count in the number below?

Answer

30,000,000,000,000

WORD PLAY

How many words can you make out of the word

CYTOSKELETON

WHAT IS THIS?

Look at the images and write down what they are and where they are in the Cells chapter. Try and remember where they are. If you get stuck, flip through the pages and see if you can find out where they are, then commit them to memory.

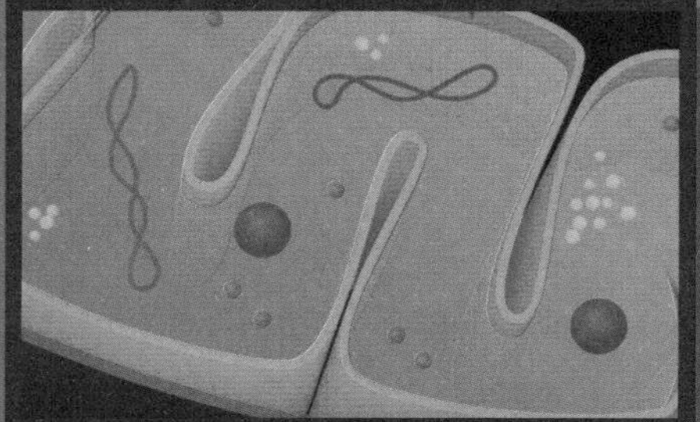

Page number

What is it?

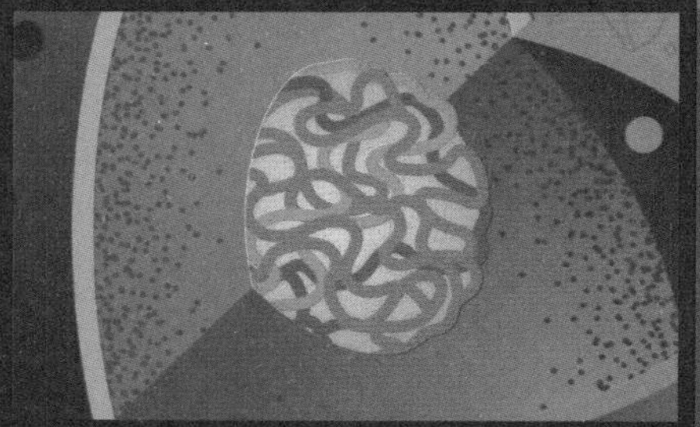

Page number

What is it?

Page number

What is it?

TEST YOURSELF!

Memorize the facts, close the book, and write down what you can remember about cells.

WORD SEARCH

Find the words that describe cells in the word s

CYTOPLASM CYTOSKELETON NUCLEUS MEMBRANE PLASMA MITOCHONDRIA

U	C	Y	T	O	P	L	A	S	M	R	F	E	C
H	H	N	L	M	P	J	L	N	P	U	I	H	Y
L	G	H	J	K	L	M	P	Q	R	M	S	U	T
F	A	N	C	B	F	L	H	Y	W	E	X	Z	O
R	M	W	B	E	R	N	D	S	X	M	K	D	S
A	S	D	O	N	B	S	U	R	S	B	T	F	K
S	A	U	I	O	X	E	K	P	P	R	S	G	E
E	L	C	F	E	L	K	M	K	S	A	D	Y	L
I	P	A	X	C	V	A	S	J	C	N	H	P	E
R	T	N	U	R	A	M	H	L	N	E	P	N	T
B	U	N	I	E	N	P	L	N	U	X	K	J	O
T	J	X	Y	E	D	X	M	O	Q	L	X	U	N
M	I	T	O	C	H	O	N	D	R	I	A	J	X
S	Q	T	V	H	O	S	O	N	J	S	L	U	I

HOW MANY?

Count how many items there are in each box and write your answer in the square provided.

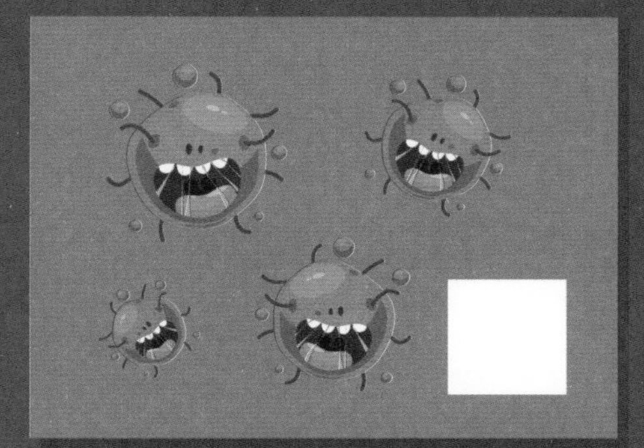
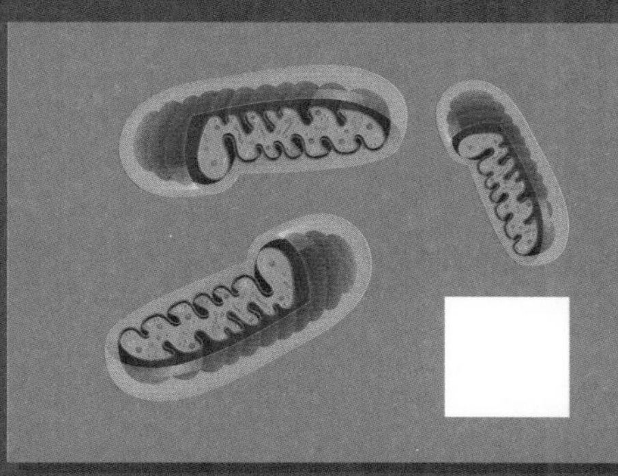

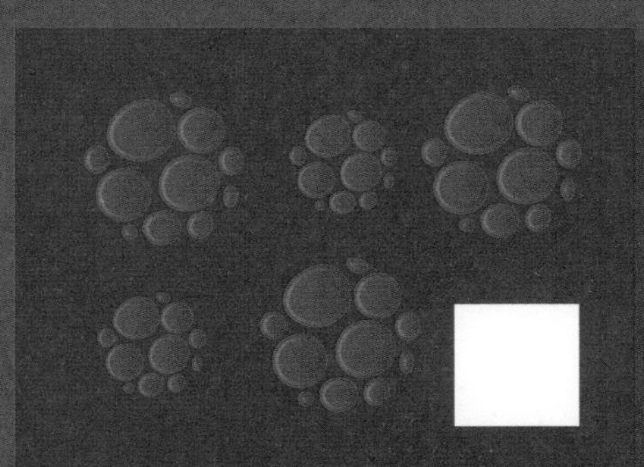
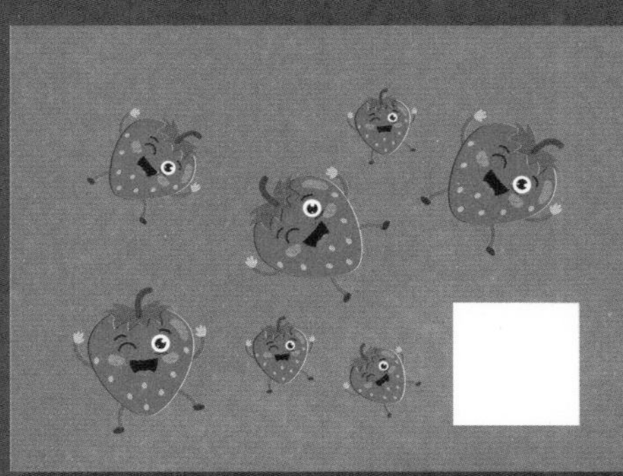
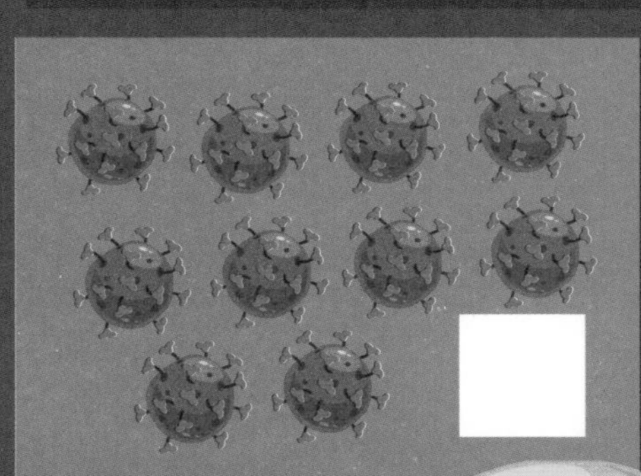

COLOR IT IN!

Viruses – which can make you feel pretty yucky – are also known as cells. Color the viruses in. Think of the times you or your friends have felt poorly. What color would you make it if you had a cold?

© Getty Images

YOUR BODY

Are you ready to meet the tissues and organs that work together to keep you alive? Your body is an incredible machine, with lots of moving parts that all do different jobs. These parts belong to ten main systems. So, before we begin, it's time for a body system countdown!

SYSTEM TEN is your circulation – a powerful pump in your chest that pushes blood to every corner of your body through lots of stretchy pipes. It delivers nutrients and oxygen to all your cells.

SYSTEM NINE is your digestive system – a tube that stretches from your mouth right down to your bottom. It takes in food at the top, sucks out all the goodness, and gets rid of the waste.

SYSTEM EIGHT is your endocrine (pronounced end-oh-cry-n) system – your hormone factory. It tells your body to grow, sleep, and make energy.

SYSTEM SEVEN is your skin – a whole system all on its own! It protects you from the outside world and helps you keep your temperature steady.

SYSTEM SIX is your immune system – your own personal army. It fights infection, helping you to get better when you feel sick.

SYSTEM FIVE is your muscular system – all the muscles that attach to your skeleton. It moves your bones, letting you walk, smile, and breathe.

SYSTEM FOUR is your nervous system – your personal computer and electrical wires. It tells your body what to do.

SYSTEM THREE is your urinary (pronounced you-rin-eh-ree) system – a filter that cleans your blood. Its whole job is to make pee!

SYSTEM TWO is your respiratory (pronounced re-spi-ra-tor-ee) system – your lungs, mouth, and nose. It brings fresh air into the body and gets rid of waste.

And finally, SYSTEM ONE is your skeletal system – your bones. It gives you your shape and lets you move.

Now that you've finished the body countdown, you're ready to meet your insides. Let's go!

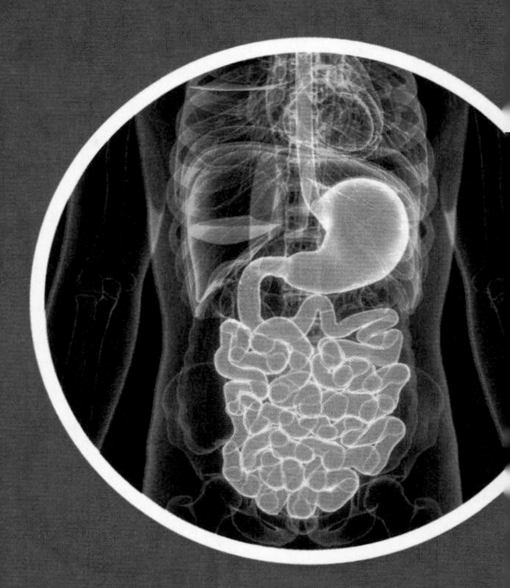

WORD SCRAMBLE

Think of some parts of the human body, and see if you can spot them in the scrambled words below. Match them to the pictures

1. KEOSTENL

2. ANBIR

3. STHOMCA

4. ENIKYD

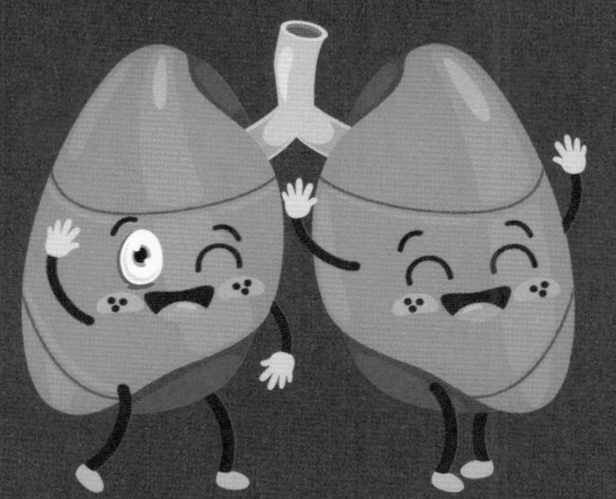

5. GNLSU

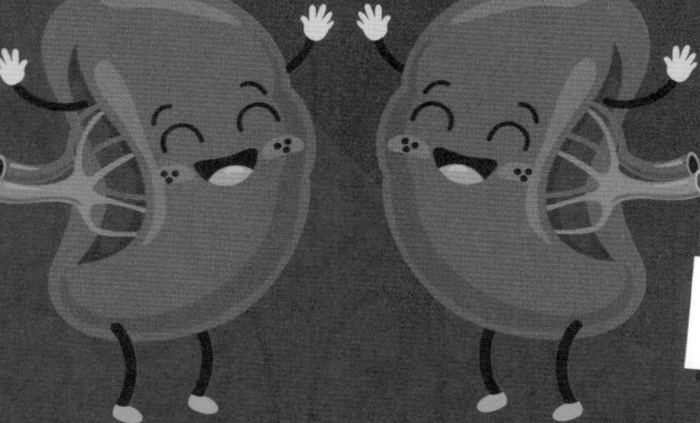

6. REAHT

ANSWERS: 1: skeleton, 2: brain, 3: stomach, 4: kidney, 5: lungs, 6: heart

THE BRAIN: THE COMPUTER IN YOUR HEAD

Your brain is the most powerful machine that nature has ever invented. It controls almost everything about your body, from the movement of your arms and legs, to the speed of your heart, and even your temperature. It is a supercomputer inside your head!

It has three main jobs to do: some of them you probably know about, but others happen without you realizing.

Your brain's first job is to manage your thoughts, emotions, and senses. This happens in the very outside part of your brain, in an area called the cerebrum (pronounced seh-ree-brum). There are trillions of brain cells here! Each one connects to thousands of others, and they are always passing messages back and forth.

The cerebrum is the biggest part of your brain, and it's the one that makes you different from other animals. It's the part of the brain that makes humans really clever. Have a look at the picture on this page to find out what each part of the cerebrum does.

Your brain's second job is controlling your conscious movements – the ones you decide to do. These include walking, running, waving, smiling, and talking. This job happens at the back of your brain, in an area called the cerebellum (pronounced se-re-bell-um). The cerebellum tells your muscles what to do, and it makes sure that they all work together in the right order.

Your brain's third, and most important, job is to keep you alive! It happens in the very middle of your brain, in an area called the brainstem. This part of your brain controls your breathing and heartbeat, makes you sleep and wake up, and it tells the muscles in your gut to digest your food. Imagine if you had to think about all of that yourself!

FRONTAL LOBE

HOW YOU PRONOUNCE MY NAME: frun-tul lobe

I HELP YOU TO... THINK

This is the part of your brain that you think with. You use it to make choices and plan for the future.

TEMPORAL LOBE

HOW YOU PRONOUNCE MY NAME: tem-poor-ul lobe

I HELP YOU TO... LISTEN AND REMEMBER

This is the part of your brain that handles words. It works out what you are hearing and helps you to learn.

SPINAL CORD

HOW YOU PRONOUNCE MY NAME: spy-nul cord

I HELP YOU TO... TALK TO YOUR BODY

This is the group of nerves that connect your brain to the rest of your body. They pass messages up and down your spine.

FIVE THINGS YOU NEED TO KNOW ABOUT YOUR BRAIN

1 YOUR BRAIN HAS BILLIONS OF CELLS

There are eighty-six billion nerve cells inside your brain, and the same number of helper cells!

2 YOUR BRAIN IS VERY LIGHT!

Your brain weighs three pounds–about the same as a bag and a half of flour.

3 YOUR BRAIN IS MULTICOLORED

The outside of your brain looks pink, but inside it is gray and white.

4 YOUR BRAIN SAVES ENERGY

Your brain uses about the same amount of energy as a lightbulb – only twenty watts!

5 YOUR BRAIN ISN'T THE BIGGEST

Humans might be the smartest animals, but whales, dolphins, and elephants all have larger brains.

PARIETAL LOBE

HOW YOU PRONOUNCE MY NAME: puh-ry-et-ul lobe

I HELP YOU TO...

FEEL

This is the part of your brain that looks after your senses. It thinks about touch, pressure, pain, heat, and cold.

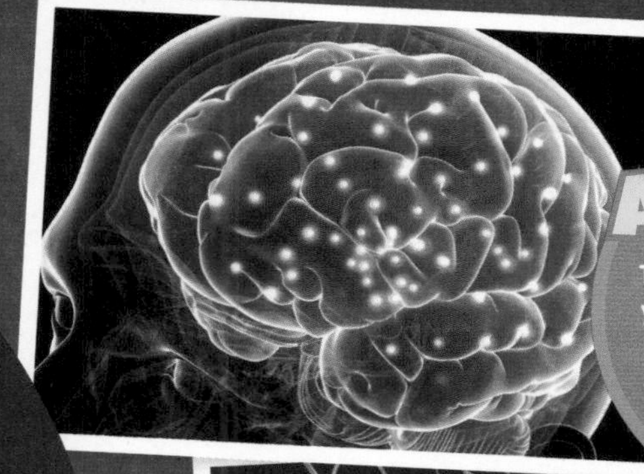

THINK ABOUT IT!

Think of all of the activities you do at home, outdoors, or at school. Which part of the brain are you using to do those things?

CEREBELLUM

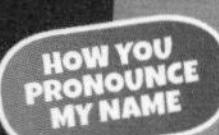

se-re-bell-um

I HELP YOU TO...

MOVE

This is the part of your brain that makes your muscles move. It controls your arms and legs, and also your face and eyes.

OCCIPITAL LOBE

ok-sip-it-ul lobe

I HELP YOU TO...

SEE

This is the part of your brain that shows you what the world looks like. It turns the messages from your eyes into pictures.

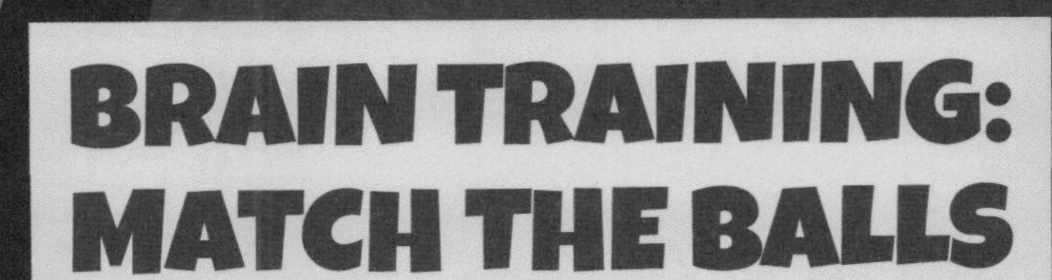

BRAIN TRAINING: MATCH THE BALLS

What order do the balls need to be in to match the picture above it?

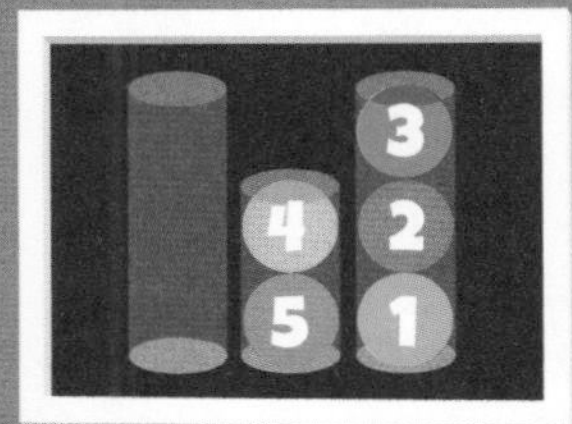

© Getty Images

NERVOUS SYSTEM: HELPING YOU FEEL AND SENSE

Your nervous system controls your whole body. It sends messages to and from your brain along cells that work a lot like wires.

These cells, called nerve cells, have three parts: a cell body, dendrites (pronounced den-dryts), and an axon (pronounced aks-on).

The cell body is in the middle, and it looks like most ordinary cells. It has a nucleus, and all the machinery that a cell needs to stay alive.

The dendrites are on one side, and they look a bit like the branches of a tree. Their job is to listen out for messages from other nerve cells.

The axon is on the other side, and it looks like a long, thin wire. Its job is to pass messages on to the next set of nerve cells.

When the dendrites hear a message from another nerve cell, they set off a wave of electricity that passes through the cell body and along the axon. When that wave gets to the end of the axon, the nerve cell lets out a great puff of chemicals. These chemicals float along to the next nerve cell, passing the message to its dendrites. This sets off another wave of electricity.

There are lots of different types of nerve cells in your nervous system, but they do two main jobs. The first job is to control your voluntary movements, like running, jumping, and talking. The second job is to control the inside of your body; your heartbeat, digestion, and breathing.

The group of nerves that control your movement is called the somatic (pronounced so-mat-ick) nervous system. It passes messag from your brain to your muscles, telling them when to contract and when to relax.

The group of nerves that control the inside of your body is called the autonomic nervous system (pronounced or-toe-nom-ick). It passes messages from your brain to your organs.

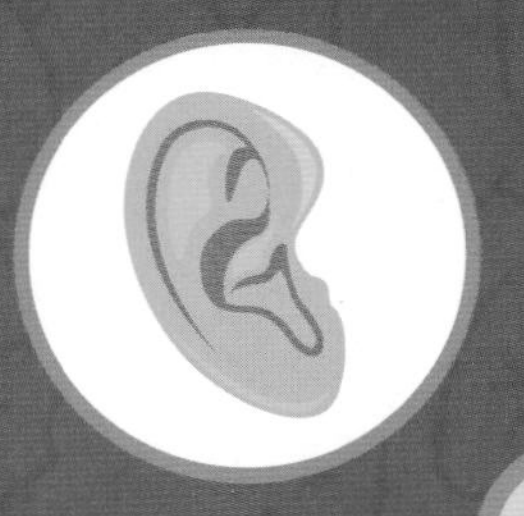

BRAIN

HOW YOU PRONOUNCE MY NAME: brayn

I HELP YOU TO...

THINK AND FEEL

Your brain is the control center of your nervous system. It listens out for messages from the body and sends messages back.

WATCH THIS!

ANATOMY OF THE SPINAL CORD

SCAN WITH YOUR PHONE OR TABLET

https://bit.ly/3rTdLDn

SPINAL CORD

HOW YOU PRONOUNCE MY NAME: spy-nal cord

I HELP YOU TO...

SEND MESSAGES FROM YOUR BRAIN TO YOUR BODY

This bundle of nerves is inside your spine. It is the main highway for information traveling to and from your brain.

NERVES

HOW YOU PRONOUNCE MY NAME: nerv

I HELP YOU TO...

SENSE AND MOVE

Thousands of nerves travel to and from your spinal cord. They connect every corner of your body to your brain.

UNSCRAMBLE THE WORDS

Unscramble the words to reveal some things about the nervous system. How do you pronounce them?

1 ROCD ALSPIN

2 RAINB

3 Revne

4 Neess

5 NOXA

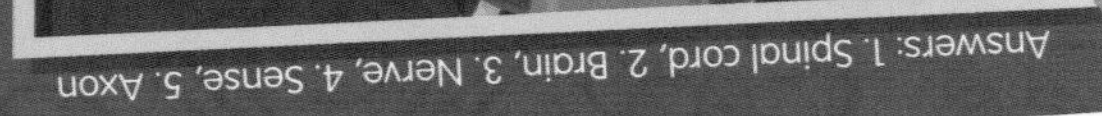

Answers: 1. Spinal cord, 2. Brain, 3. Nerve, 4. Sense, 5. Axon

WATCH THIS!

DISCOVER MORE ABOUT YOUR BRAIN

SCAN WITH YOUR PHONE OR TABLET

https://bit.ly/3ftufgr

TRY IT OUT!

React without your brain!

WHAT YOU'LL NEED

- A friend
- A chair

INSTRUCTIONS

1. GRAB A CHAIR
   Sit on a chair with your legs crossed.
2. RELAX A LEG
   Make sure your top leg is completely relaxed.
3. FIND YOUR SOFT SPOT
   Find the soft space just under your kneecap.
4. GET A FRIEND TO HELP
   Ask your friend to give it a quick tap with the side of their hand.

WHAT HAVE YOU LEARNED?

Did your leg kick out all on its own? That's your knee-jerk reflex! It's amazing because it happens without your brain. The nerves in your knee sense the tap and send a message to your spinal cord. Your spinal cord sends a message straight back to the muscles in your leg, making you kick without asking your brain first!

© Getty Images

DIGESTIVE SYSTEM: HOW YOUR BODY DEALS WITH FOOD

QUIZ

HOW WELL DO YOU KNOW YOUR DIGESTIVE SYSTEM?

WHICH PART OF YOUR DIGESTIVE SYSTEM MAKES ACID?

WHERE DO DIGESTIVE ENZYMES COME FROM?

WHAT DOES THE GALLBLADDER MAKE?

WHICH TUBE GETS ALL THE GOODNESS OUT OF YOUR FOOD?

WHICH TUBE MAKES WASTE?

ANSWERS: Stomach, Pancreas, Bile, Small intestine, Large intestine

Your digestive system is thirty feet long! It's a big, hollow tube that travels all the way from your mouth to your bottom, with lots of twists and turns in between. It's busy every hour of the day, breaking down the food you eat and turning it into energy and nutrients for your cells.

Your digestive system starts working as soon as you even think about food. You can feel it! If you imagine your favorite meal, your mouth will start to water. That's saliva, a special kind of liquid that helps to make your food easier to swallow.

When you start chewing, your mouth will make even more saliva, working with your teeth and tongue to turn every mouthful into a slippery ball that can slide down your throat.

When you swallow a mouthful of food, it passes into a tube called the esophagus (pronounced oh-sof-a-gus). This tube squeezes the mouthful down through your neck, between your lungs, and into your stomach.

Your stomach is under your ribs on the left-hand side. It's about the size of your fist when empty, but can expand like a balloon to hold a whole meal and a few glasses of water. It churns food together, mixing it with acid and enzymes to make a paste.

When your dinner is almost completely smooth, your stomach starts to squirt it into your intestines a little at a time.

First, it passes through your small intestine, which finishes breaking your food down and gets all the nutrients and energy out. This takes hours!

Then it travels through your large intestine, which sucks out all the water, leaving behind solid brown waste. This takes even longer, often more than a day!

Finally, when all the digestion is done, it's time to go to the toilet.

BIG NUMBERS

800ML

Your pancreas makes 800 milliliters (1.4 pints) of digestive juices every day.

36 HOURS

It takes up to three days for your food to move through your large intestine.

4,000ML

Your stomach can stretch to hold 4,000 milliliters of food and drink.

2,000 LBS

The average American eats 2,000 pounds of food a year.

1 DOWN THE ESOPHAGUS

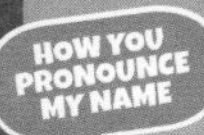

oh-sof-a-gus

I HELP YOU TO...

SWALLOW YOUR FOOD

The first step on the journey through your digestive system is a slippery slide down your esophagus. This stretchy tube pushes food from your mouth to your stomach.

2 INTO THE STOMACH

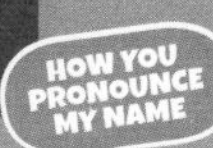

stuh-mak

I HELP YOU TO...

BREAK YOUR FOOD INTO TINY PIECES

When food gets to the end of the esophagus, it drops into the stomach. This bag full of acid and enzymes churns your food to make a paste.

3 THROUGH TO THE SMALL INTESTINE

HOW YOU PRONOUNCE MY NAME

in-tes-tin

I HELP YOU TO...

GET THE GOODNESS OUT OF YOUR FOOD

Once your food is all squashed up, it's ready to start its long journey through the small intestine. This tube absorbs energy and nutrients.

4 MIX WITH BILE FROM THE GALLBLADDER

HOW YOU PRONOUNCE MY NAME

gorl-blad-er

I HELP YOU TO...

STOP YOUR STOMACH ACID

Your gallbladder squirts your food with a green liquid called bile. This breaks big blobs of fat into smaller pieces.

5 SQUIRT WITH ENZYMES FROM THE PANCREAS

HOW YOU PRONOUNCE MY NAME

pan-kree-yas

I HELP YOU TO...

BREAK YOUR FOOD INTO EVEN TINIER PIECES

Your pancreas squirts your food with enzymes. These break big molecules down into nutrients that your small intestine can absorb.

6 OUT THROUGH THE LARGE INTESTINE

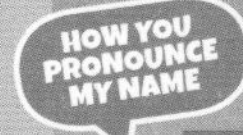

in-tes-tin

I HELP YOU TO...

GET RID OF THE WASTE

The last step is a trip through the large intestine. This tube sucks all the water out of your food and gets rid of the waste.

TEST YOURSELF 3

Memorize the facts, close the book, and write them down. How many can you remember and jot down in three minutes?

© Getty Images

HOW YOU SEE

Your eyes work almost exactly like cameras! They have an opening that lets the light in, a lens that focuses the light, and sensors that make the picture.

When light hits an object, some of the rays disappear inside it, and others bounce off. Some of these bouncing rays hit your eyes, and that's what lets you see the object.

The first thing the light hits is the cornea (pronounced cor-nee-ya). It is a see-through tissue on the front of your eye. Its job is to bend the light in towards your pupil.

Your pupil is the black part right in the middle of your eye. It's surrounded by a colorful ring called the iris. Light passes through the pupil and into another see-through tissue called the lens.

The job of the lens is to bend the light so that it hits the sensors at the back of the eye. How much the light needs to bend depends on how far away the object is. The lens is stretchy, a bit like a gummy candy. This means that it can change shape. It gets short and fat to bend light more, helping you to see nearby objects, and it gets long and thin to bend light less, helping you to see objects far away.

There are two types of light sensor in the back of your eye: cells called rods, and cells called cones. When light hits them, they get excited and start sending messages to your brain.

The rods get excited by any kind of light, but the cones only get excited by certain colors. Some like red, others like green, and the rest like blue.

Your brain listens out for these messages, and uses them to make pictures. The red, green, and blue messages mix to make all the other colors in the rainbow!

IRIS

HOW YOU PRONOUNCE MY NAME

i-ris

MY MAIN JOB:

CONTROLLING HOW MUCH LIGHT GETS INTO YOUR EYE

I am the colorful part of your eye. Depending on your genes, I can be brown, hazel, green, grey, or blue. I have tiny muscles that make me bigger or smaller to change the amount of light that gets into your eye.

LENS

HOW YOU PRONOUNCE MY NAME

lens

MY MAIN JOB:

BENDING LIGHT ONTO THE RETINA

I am like the lens in a pair of glasses, except I can change shape! It is my job to bend the light so that it all hits the back of your eye in the same place. This is called "focusing." I make sure the pictures you see are sharp and not blurry.

RETINA

HOW YOU PRONOUNCE MY NAME

ret-in-ah

MY MAIN JOB:

DETECTING LIGHT

I am the back of your eye. I am covered in tiny light sensors called rods and cones. These sensors switch on when light hits them. Rods turn on for any light, and help you see in black and white. Cones turn on for red, green, or blue light, and help you see in color.

PUPIL

HOW YOU PRONOUNCE MY NAME

pyoo-pil

MY MAIN JOB:

LETTING LIGHT INTO YOUR EYE

I am the black hole at the front of your eye. It is my job to let light in. The iris makes me bigger when you're in the dark, and smaller when you're in bright light.

CORNEA

HOW YOU PRONOUNCE MY NAME

cor-nee-ya

MY MAIN JOB:

BENDING LIGHT INTO THE EYE

I am like the window on the very front of your eye. I cover the iris and the pupil. It is my job to bend the light that hits your eye, making sure that it goes through your pupil.

SCLERA

HOW YOU PRONOUNCE MY NAME

skl-e-ra

MY MAIN JOB:

PROTECTING YOUR EYE

I am the white part of your eye. I am very strong, and it is my job to keep your eye safe. I cover almost all of your eyeball, from the front to the very back.

FIVE THINGS YOU NEED TO KNOW ABOUT YOUR EYES

BLINKS ARE SUPER FAST

It takes one tenth of a second to complete a blink – that's 100 milliseconds.

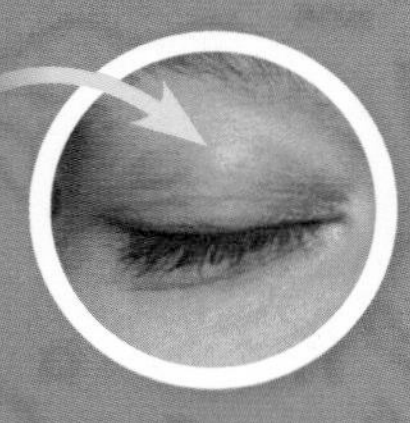

TEARS ARE SALTY

Your tears are mostly water with a bit of salt, oil, and protein.

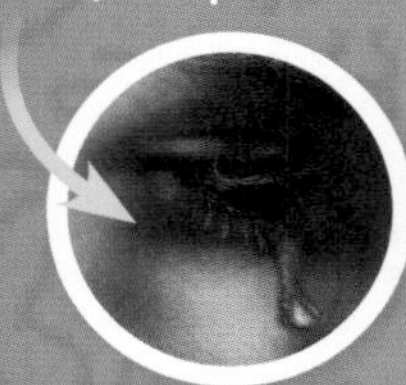

EYEBROWS ARE NATURE'S UMBRELLAS

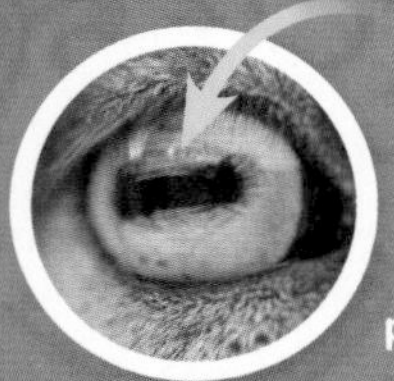

Your eyebrows help to keep sweat and rain out of your eyes.

YOU BLINK A LOT

On average, you blink between fifteen and twenty times every single minute.

SOME ANIMALS DON'T HAVE ROUND PUPILS

Cats have slit-shaped pupils, and goat pupils are rectangles!

TRY IT OUT!

Test your pupils!

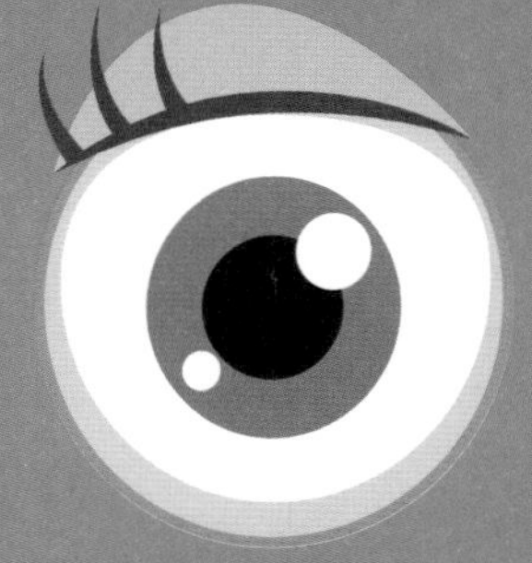

WHAT YOU'LL NEED

- Magnifying glass
- Mirror
- Flashlight

INSTRUCTIONS

1. MAFNIFYING GLASS
Put the magnifying glass on the mirror.
2. TAKE A LOOK
Look into the middle of it with one eye.
3. WHAT DO YOU SEE?
Can you see your pupil and your iris?
4. FLASHLIGHT
Now, ask a grown-up to shine a flashlight in your eye.
5. RESULTS
What happens?
6. LIGHTS OFF
Now, try turning all the lights off.
7. WHAT HAPPENS?
What happens to your iris and your pupil now?

WHAT HAVE YOU LEARNED?

You might have noticed your pupil changing size. When it's bright, your pupil gets very small. This stops too much light from getting into your eye. When it's dim, your pupil gets very big. This lets more light in so that you can still see in the dark.

OPTIC NERVE

HOW YOU PRONOUNCE MY NAME: op-tik nerve

MY MAIN JOB: SENDING MESSAGES TO THE BRAIN

I am the wire that connects your eye to your brain! I collect all the signals from the rods and cones, and send them right to the back of your head. Your brain turns those signals into a picture.

Look at the picture below. Can you see it moving?

OPTICAL ILLUSIONS

© Getty Images

YOUR EARS: HOW YOU HEAR SOUNDS

Your ears pick up vibrations in the air molecules around your head and turn them into electrical signals. Your brain turns those signals into sounds.

You can hear vibrations between fifty Hz and 20,000 Hz, letting you listen to the rumble of thunder, the buzz of a mosquito's wings, and everything in between. But how do your ears work?

The outside of your ear, called the pinna (pronounced pin-er), catches noises like a satellite dish. It sends them into your ear canal, the hole on the side of your head. Deep inside that hole, a piece of tissue called the eardrum starts to wobble.

On the other side of the eardrum, three tiny bones start to wobble too. Their job is to pass the wobbles to the cochlea (pronounced cok-lee-ya), which looks a lot like a snail shell.

The cochlea is full of fluid, which starts to move when the ear bones wobble. That movement rocks tiny hairs, making them bend backwards and forwards. As those hairs bend, they open little gates in the cells underneath them. This creates electricity!

The cochlea passes that electricity into a bundle of nerves called the cochlear nerve. This sends messages to a part of your brain called the auditory cortex (pronounced or-dit-or-ee cor-teks). The brain cells here work out how loud the sound is and whether its pitch is high or a low.

Your hearing is quite good, but it's not the best in nature. Whales and elephants can hear much lower-pitched sounds than we can, picking up frequencies as low as seven Hz. Dolphins and bats can hear extremely high-pitched noises, known as ultrasound, with frequencies up to 100,000 Hz. If you want to find out how good your ears are, try watching some of the videos on this page!

TRUE OR FALSE?

Write next to the statements whether the information about ears and hearing is true or false.

THE COCHLEA IS THE SHAPE OF A SNAIL SHELL — TRUE ☐ OR FALSE ☐

THE EAR BONES BANG ON THE EARDRUM — TRUE ☐ OR FALSE ☐

EARS TURN SOUND INTO ELECTRICITY — TRUE ☐ OR FALSE ☐

WHY DO MY EARS MAKE ME DIZZY?

Your ears contain your balance sensors, three tubes called the semi-circular canals. Each one points in a different direction, and they are all full of fluid. That fluid sloshes around when you move, helping your brain to work out which way your head is facing. When you spin around and then stop, the fluid keeps moving, which can make you feel dizzy.

TYMPANIC MEMBRANE

HOW YOU PRONOUNCE MY NAME

tim-pan-ik mem-brayn

MY MAIN JOB

TO WOBBLE WHEN SOUNDS HIT ME

I am the eardrum! I am a sheet of tissue a bit like skin. I separate the inside of your ear from the outside. When sounds hit me, I start to wobble. Those wobbles make it possible for you to hear.

MALLEUS, INCUS, AND STAPES

mal-ee-yus, in-kus, stay-pees

MY MAIN JOB

PASSING SOUNDS INTO THE EAR

We are the ear bones, the three smallest bones in your body! We are shaped like a hammer, an anvil, and a stirrup. It is our job to pass wobbles from the eardrum to the cochlea.

COCHLEAR NERVE

HOW YOU PRONOUNCE MY NAME

ok-lee-yar nerv

MY MAIN JOB

TO PASS MESSAGES TO YOUR BRAIN

I take electrical signals from the cochlea and pass them on to the brain. I contain around 30,000 nerve cells! They connect to the hairs in the cochlea, waiting for messages to send to the brain.

COCHLEA

cok-lee-ya

MY MAIN JOB

TURNING SOUND INTO ELECTRICITY

I am a tube inside the ear, and I'm shaped like a snail shell. I'm full of fluid and tiny hairs. The ear bones make my fluid shake. That bends the hairs and makes electrical signals.

WATCH THIS!

SCAN WITH YOUR PHONE OR TABLET

GUESS THE SOUND!

Mr. Teach has put together twenty sounds. Can you guess what they are?
https://bit.ly/3i8n66Z

HEAR YOUR HEART

Ever wondered what your heart sounds like? Medzcool has made a video.
https://bit.ly/3BNXWlI

GUESS THE SONG

Test your ears with this cartoon theme song guessing game from TopSpot Animation.
https://bit.ly/2VdQeR9

DO YOU HAVE SUPERHUMAN HEARING?

Test your hearing with this fun video from Bright Side.
https://bit.ly/3ycOJBj

© Getty Images

SMELLING AND TASTING

Your sense of smell and taste are different, but they work closely together. You need both senses at once to enjoy your favorite foods!

Your main taste sense organ is your tongue. It's a muscle, which is why you can move it in all different directions to eat, speak, and sing. Use that muscle to stick your tongue out, and go and look at it in the mirror. What can you see?

You probably noticed lots of tiny bumps. Scientists call them papillae (pronounced pa-pill-ee). If you touch them, you'll notice that they feel a bit rough. They help your tongue to grip on to your food when you're eating.

What you might not see, or feel, is what's hiding underneath: your taste buds!

Taste buds are special groups of cells that can sense chemicals in your food. You have about 10,000 of them! They can detect five main types of taste: sweet, salty, sour, bitter, and umami.

Try the taste experiment on this page to see how good you are at tasting.

You might wonder how foods can taste so different if there are only five kinds of taste. It's because most of what we think of as taste is actually smell!

Your nose has around twelve million smell-sensing cells. These cells are covered in tiny hairs that can sense chemicals in the air. They can detect around 10,000 different chemicals. That lets you tell the difference between around a trillion smells!

Lots of smells get into your nose through your nostrils, but when you're eating, they get in through the back of your throat too. Your brain mixes the smell signals with the signals from your tongue, and that's what makes your food taste good.

CIRCUMVALLATE PAPILLAE

HOW YOU PRONOUNCE MY NAME

sir-cum-va-late pa-pill-ee

You can find me right at the back of your tongue. I have thousands of taste buds that send messages to your brain as you're swallowing.

FIVE THINGS YOU NEED TO KNOW ABOUT SMELLING AND TASTING

1 YOU CAN SMELL FEAR

People make a special kind of sweat when they're frightened

2 YOU CAN'T SEE YOUR TASTE BUDS

The bumps on your tongue are not your taste buds! They are too small to see.

3 DOGS SMELL BETTER THAN US

Dogs have around 220 million smell-sensing cells in their noses!

4 ALL OF YOUR TONGUE SENSES ALL TASTES

Don't let anyone tell you that different parts of your tongue taste different things!

5 SOME PEOPLE ARE SUPERTASTERS

If you're one of them, you might find bitter foods taste really, really bitter.

FUNGIFORM PAPILLAE

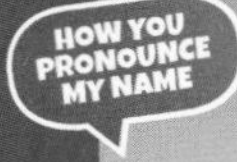

fun-gee-form pa-pill-ee

It means that I look like a mushroom! I am all over the very front of the tongue, and I am often red in color. I have lots of taste buds.

LEARN MORE!

SCAN WITH YOUR PHONE OR TABLET

https://bit.ly/3lUUfFC

WHICH FOODS LINK TO HOW THEY TASTE?

FOLIATE PAPILLAE

fo-lee-ate pa-pill-ee

I look like folds on the sides of your tongue, near to your back teeth. There are about twenty of me, and we contain hundreds of taste buds each.

WHAT DO YOU THINK?

Smell and taste a selection of foods that you have at home. Do they taste as they smell? Write the items down and record your findings.

TRY IT OUT!

WHAT YOU'LL NEED

- A sweet food, like sugar
- A salty food, like salt
- A sour food, like lemon juice
- A bitter food, like cocoa powder
- A blindfold

INSTRUCTIONS

1. COVER YOUR EYES
   Put on your blindfold, hold your nose, and open your mouth.
2. TASTE TEST
   Ask someone to put a little bit of one of the foods on your tongue.
3. WHAT IS IT?
   Can you tell which food you're eating?
4. WHAT DOES IT TASTE LIKE?
   Can you tell whether it is sweet, sour, salty, or bitter?

WHAT HAVE YOU LEARNED?

Working out which food is which is really hard when you hold your nose! Most of your sense of taste is really your sense of smell. You might have found it easier to decide if the food was sweet, sour, salty, or bitter. That's the job your tongue does best.

TASTE TEST!

What does cilantro taste like?

WHAT YOU'LL NEED

- Fresh cilantro
- Some friends

INSTRUCTIONS

1. TRY IT
   Each chew a cilantro leaf.
2. WHAT DOES IT TASTE LIKE?
   Write down what you think it tastes like.

WHAT HAVE YOU LEARNED?

Did anyone write down "soap"? Cilantro contains chemicals called aldehydes (pronounced al-du-hides). Lots of people who think that cilantro tastes like soap have a gene that makes them extra sensitive to these chemicals. It changes their sense of smell, which changes the way that cilantro tastes.

© Getty Images, Alamy

YOUR SKIN: YOUR BIGGEST ORGAN

Your skin is the biggest organ in your body! When you're finished growing, it will measure twenty-two square feet! Its job is to protect you from the outside world, making sure nothing harmful gets into your body, and nothing important gets out.

If you looked at your skin under a microscope, you would find layer upon layer of cells. It's like microscopic armor.

The bottom layer is called the hypodermis (pronounced hi-po-dur-miss). Hypo means "under" and dermis means "skin." This layer is full of fat, which helps to keep you warm, and tissue, which holds all your cells together.

The next layer is the dermis. This is where you'll find your hairs and sweat glands.

You have around five million hairs on your body, and only 100,000 of those are on your head! The rest are all over your skin. They lift up when you're cold, helping to trap a layer of warm air.

Your sweat glands are everywhere too, but you'll find most of them in your armpits, on the palms of your hands, and on the soles of your feet. You have two to four million in total!

Sweat glands make sweat when you're hot. It turns into steam in the air and floats away, taking some of your extra body heat with it.

The very top layer of your skin is the epidermis (pronounced eh-pee-dur-miss). Epi means "on top." This is where your skin cells are, stacked up in layers, like a brick wall. The cells at the bottom of the wall are alive and growing, but the cells at the top are dead.

It's the dead cells that keep your body safe. They brush off whenever you touch something, so the cells underneath divide constantly to keep the barrier fresh. Most of the dust you see around your house is old skin!

TEST YOURSELF

Memorize the facts, close the book, and write them down. How many can you remember and jot down in five minutes?

QUIZ

1. HOW MANY LAYERS DOES THE SKIN HAVE?

2. WHAT TEMPERATURE SHOULD THE BODY BE?

3. HOW MANY SWEAT GLANDS DO YOU HAVE?

4. WHAT IS DUST MADE OF?

5. HOW DOES THE SKIN COOL THE BODY DOWN?

ANSWERS: 1. Three, 2. 98.6 degrees Fahrenheit, 3. Four million, 4. Skin cells, 5. Sweating

WHY IS MY SKIN IMPORTANT?

IT PROTECTS YOU AGAINST MICROBES

Your skin is your body's first line of defense against germs. It stops bacteria and viruses from getting into your body. Have you ever noticed how fast your skin fixes itself when you have a cut or a graze? Your immune system rushes to fix the injury to stop anything nasty getting in.

IT KEEPS YOUR TEMPERATURE STEADY

Your body works best at 98.6 degrees Fahrenheit. If you get too hot or cold, your cells and molecules stop working. Your skin works a bit like a radiator, letting extra heat out when you get too warm.

IT TELLS YOU WHAT'S GOING ON AROUND YOU

Your skin is full of nerve endings! Some sense touch, like stroking or stretching. Some sense hot and cold, and some sense chemicals. These nerve endings tell you what's happening around your body, and they warn you when something hurts.

IT STORES ENERGY AND KEEPS YOU WARM

The body stores fat under the skin. It acts as a blanket to keep you warm. It also makes sure that you have spare energy in case there's a day when you don't manage to eat enough food. In your hands and feet, fat also works as a shock absorber.

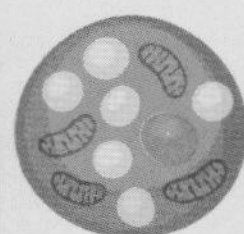

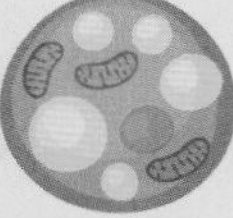

SWEAT DROP CHESS

Move the sweat drop so that it lands on each of the squares on the board, arriving back at the starting point. If you get stuck, you'll need to start again! You can't move diagonally, just left, right, forwards, and backwards.

WATCH THIS!

LEARN WHY WE SWEAT

SCAN WITH YOUR PHONE OR TABLET

https://bit.ly/2TWkvnn

© Getty Images

YOUR MUSCLES: THE TISSUES THAT MAKE YOU MOVE

WATCH THIS!
HOW YOUR MUSCLES WOR
SCAN WITH YOUR PHONE OR TABLET
https://bit.ly/2VHUnNm

You have hundreds of muscles in your body. They move everything, from your arms and legs to your eyes and lips, and even your heart and digestive system!

Most of your muscles are attached to your bones. This means that when they contract, they can move your joints. But muscles can only pull – they can't push – so they have to work in pairs. If one muscle pulls a joint in one direction, the other muscle has to pull it back again.

You can test this for yourself with your arm. When you bend your elbow, the muscle in the front of your upper arm contracts. You might even be able to see it moving! When you straighten your elbow, that muscle relaxes, and the muscle at the back of your upper arm contracts instead.

The biggest muscle in your body is the gluteus maximus (pronounced gloo-tee-yus maks-im-us), the muscle on your bottom. Its job is to hold you upright. The smallest muscle in your body is the stapedius (pronounced sta-pee-dee-yus), a muscle in your ear. It works with your smallest bone to help you hear.

These muscles, and all the others, are made from special tissues that can change length. When your muscles contract, the tissues get shorter. When your muscles relax, the tissues get longer. This is because muscles contain really weird cells!

Muscle cells are made from lots of cells joined together. They are very, very long, and have more than one nucleus. Inside, they contain thousands of tiny protein threads, all lined up in neat rows.

When a muscle contracts, these threads pull on each other, and they all bunch up. When a muscle relaxes, the threads let go of each other, and the opposite muscle pulls them all back to normal again.

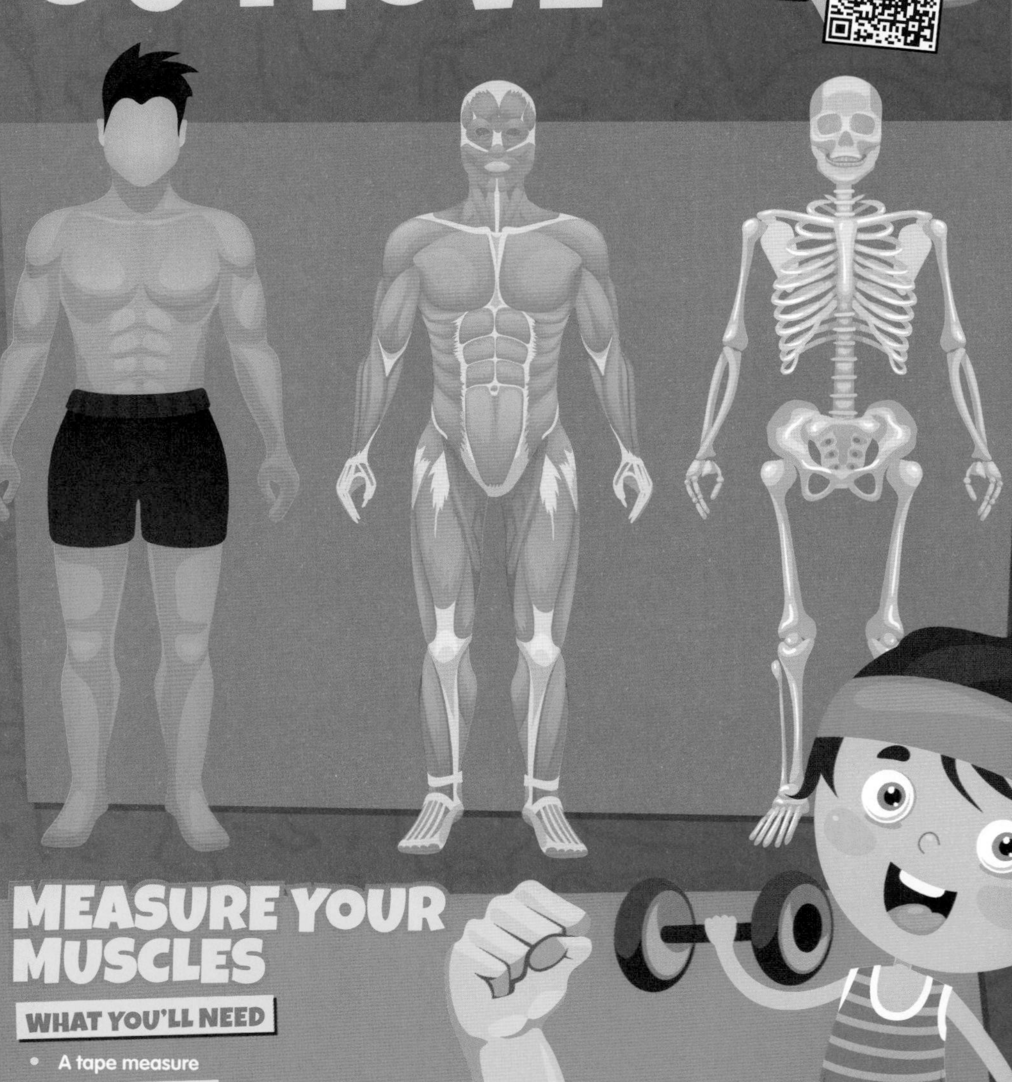

MEASURE YOUR MUSCLES

WHAT YOU'LL NEED

- A tape measure

INSTRUCTIONS

1. Relax your arm, and wrap a tape measure around the top part.
2. Take a measurement and write it down.
3. Bend your arm, and tense up the muscles.
4. Take the same measurement again.

WHAT HAVE YOU LEARNED?

Did you notice a difference between the two measurements? That's your biceps hard at work! When your arm is straight and relaxed, the biceps are long and thin. When you bend your elbow and contract that muscle, it pulls on the bone and becomes short and fat.

DIFFERENT KINDS OF MUSCLE

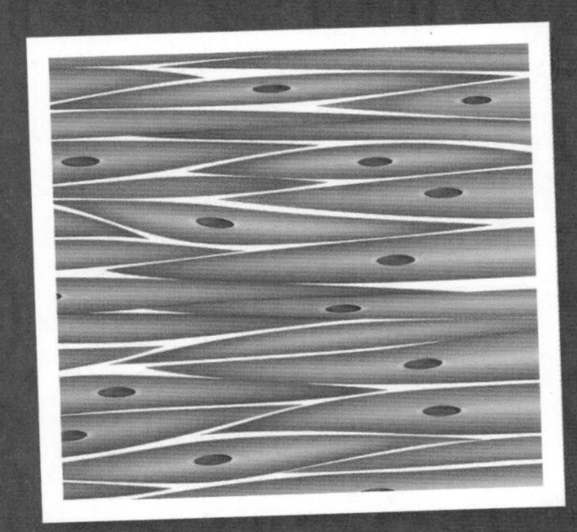

SMOOTH MUSCLE

Where I can be found in the body:
IN YOUR ORGANS

I am the type of muscle that makes your organs move. It is my job to push food through your digestive system and empty your bladder. You don't have to tell me what to do; I follow orders from your brain without you even having to think about it.

CARDIAC MUSCLE

Where I can be found in the body:
IN YOUR HEART

I am the muscle that makes your heart beat. I am very strong. I contract and relax in a rhythm to keep blood moving through your body. Unlike your skeletal muscles, I never get tired! That's important, because you need me to keep working even when you're asleep.

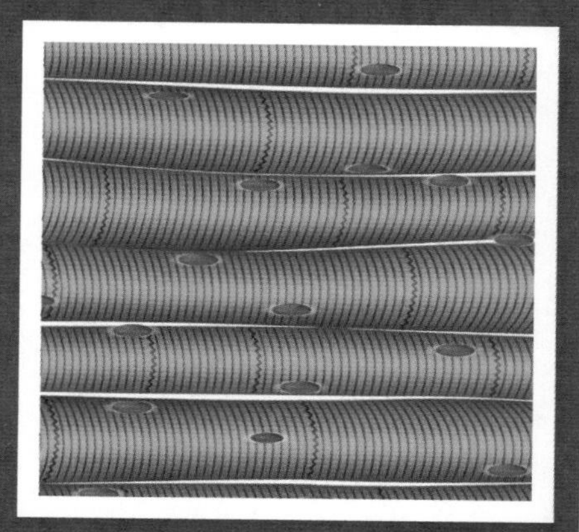

SKELETAL MUSCLE

Where I can be found in the body:
AROUND YOUR BONES

I am the type of muscle that moves your bones. There are more than 650 of me in your body! You can control me with your mind, making me contract and relax to move your body in lots of different ways.

DOT TO DOT

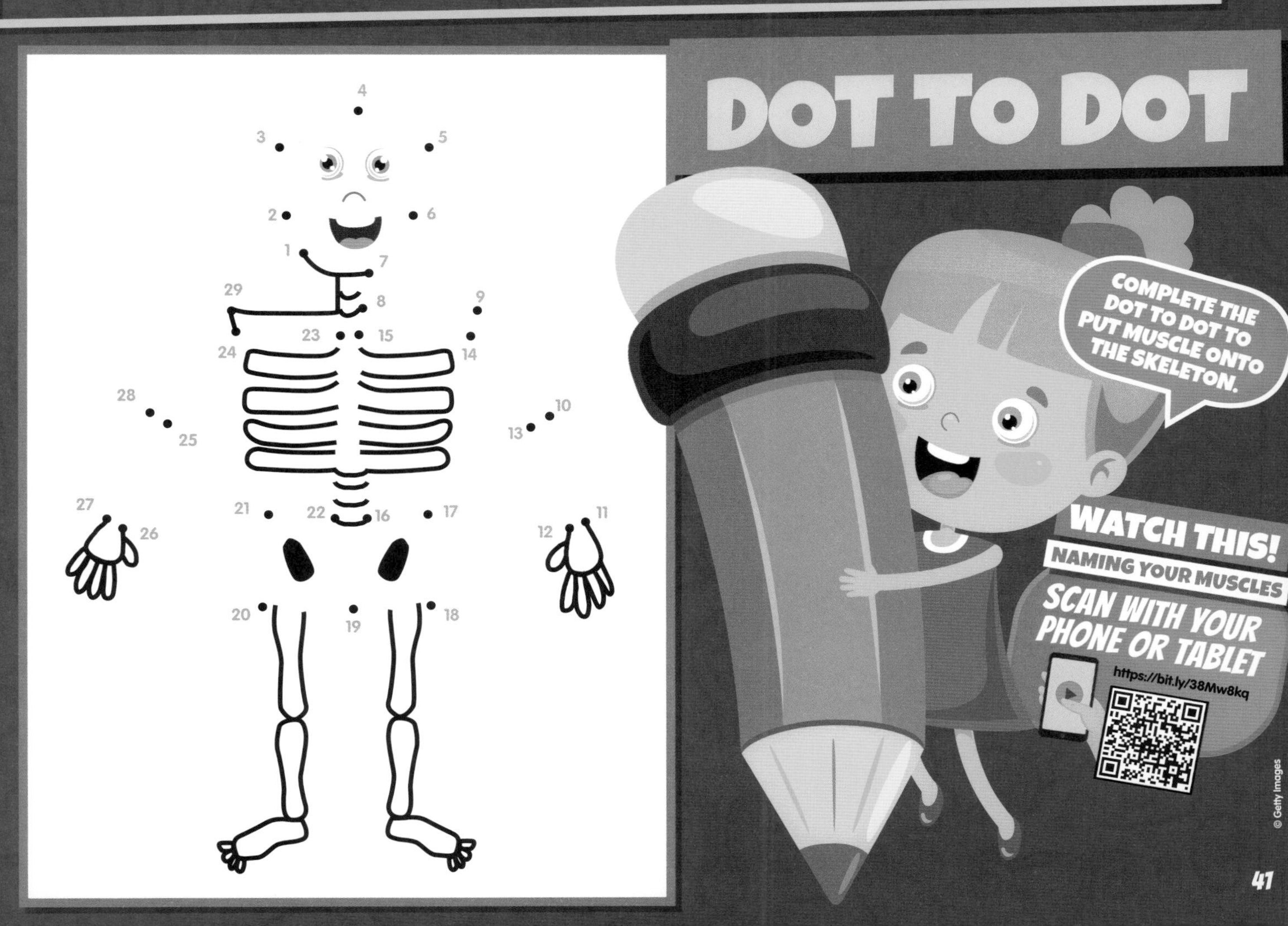

© Getty Images

YOUR HEART: PUMPING BLOOD AROUND THE BODY

Lub dub, lub dub, lub dub. That's the sound your heart makes 100,000 times a day as it pumps blood around your body!

If you looked inside your heart, you'd see four rooms called chambers. There are two small chambers at the top, called atria (pronounced ay-tree-ya), and two bigger chambers at the bottom, called ventricles (pronounced ven-tri-kuls).

Before every heartbeat, the small chambers fill up with blood. Then the heart muscle starts to squeeze.

The squeeze starts at the top of the heart, pushing the blood from the small chambers into the big chambers. As it does this, little gates between the chambers open and then snap shut. This makes the "lub" sound of the heartbeat.

The heart muscle carries on squeezing downwards, pushing the blood out of the big chambers and into two of the biggest blood vessels in the body. When this happens, another set of gates open and shut, making the "dub" sound of the heartbeat.

The reason there are four chambers is because the two sides of the heart push blood around different parts of the body. The right side of the heart collects blood from the body and pushes it to the lungs. The left side of the heart collects blood from the lungs and pushes it back out to the body.

You might remember from the page about mitochondria that all your cells need oxygen to make energy. Your blood gives them that oxygen.

If you looked at your blood under a microscope, you would see lots of tiny red cells shaped like squashed disks. Those are your red blood cells. They really like oxygen!

When they pass through your lungs, they grab all the oxygen they can carry. Then, as they travel around your body, they give that oxygen to your other cells.

Your blood also carries waste away from cells, taking carbon dioxide gas back to your lungs so you can breathe it out.

RIGHT ATRIUM

I am the small chamber at the top right of the heart. I collect blood from the body after all the oxygen has been used up. It's full of carbon dioxide. When the heart beats, I send that blood down into the right ventricle.

BIG NUMBERS

5 LITERS
You have five liters of blood in your body

45 SECONDS
It takes forty-five seconds for your blood to get all the way around your body

25 TRILLION
You have twenty-five trillion red blood cells in your body right now

35 MILLION
Your heart beats thirty-five million times a year!

WATCH THIS!

EXPLORING THE HEART

SCAN WITH YOUR PHONE OR TABLET

https://bit.ly/3fLHeKj

WATCH THIS!

LEARN MORE ABOUT YOUR BLOOD

SCAN WITH YOUR PHONE OR TABLET

https://bit.ly/3izbmKU

SPOT THE DIFFERENCE

Giving blood can help save a life. You have to be at least seventeen years old to give blood. See if you can find the four differences between these two images.

WHAT IS BLOOD TYPE?

There are four main types of blood: A, B, AB, and O. They all do the same job, but they're all a little bit different. Each person only has one type, and that type is decided by their genes.

Blood type genes decide what the outside of red blood cells looks like. People with A type blood have A molecules on their cells. People with B type blood have B molecules on their cells. People with AB type blood have both A and B molecules on their cells. And people with O type blood have neither A nor B molecules on their cells.

LEFT ATRIUM

I am the small chamber at the top left of the heart. I collect blood from the lungs. That blood is full of oxygen by the time it reaches me. When the heart beats, I pass the blood into the left ventricle.

RIGHT VENTRICLE

I am the big chamber at the bottom right of the heart. I collect blood from the right atrium. When the heart beats, I send that blood out towards the lungs. They remove the carbon dioxide and fill the red blood cells up with oxygen.

LEFT VENTRICLE

I am the biggest chamber in the heart. It's my job to push blood all the way around the body, sending oxygen to all your cells. I collect blood from the left ventricle and send it out into a huge blood vessel called the aorta (pronounced ay-or-ta).

TRY IT OUT!

How to measure your heart rate

WHAT YOU'LL NEED

- A stopwatch

INSTRUCTIONS

1. Put your fingers on the side of your neck, just under your jawbone.
2. Hold still, and see if you can feel beating.
3. Ask for help from an adult if you need to.
4. Start your stopwatch, and start counting the beats.
5. Stop when you get to fifteen seconds.
6. Write down the number of beats you counted.
7. Times that number by four

WHAT HAVE YOU LEARNED?

That number is your heart rate, the number of times your heart beats every minute. It isn't always the same; your heart beats faster when you do exercise, and slower when you're resting. That's because your body needs more oxygen when you're active. Try the experiment again after different activities, and see what you discover.

© Getty Images

YOUR BONES: THE STRONGEST PART OF YOUR BODY

Have you ever wondered what your bones look like on the inside? The answer might surprise you!

The outside of a bone is very hard. Scientists call it compact bone. It's made from solid layers of bone tissue packed closely together. But the inside is full of holes! Scientists call it spongy bone because it looks a bit like a sponge.

Both types of bone are made from the same two ingredients: collagen and minerals.

Collagen (pronounced co-la-gen) is the glue that holds your bones together. On its own, it's really bendy. Minerals are the solid chemicals that give your bones strength. On their own, they're hard but really brittle. It's the combination of collagen and minerals that makes your bones so tough.

Collagen gives bones something scientists call tensile strength. This means they don't break easily when you pull or bend them. Minerals give bones compressive strength. This means they don't squash down when they're pushed or squeezed.

You can group your bones into five types: long, short, flat, sesamoid (pronounced ses-a-moyd), and irregular bones.

Long bones are the ones in your arms and legs. They're mainly made from strong compact bone. Short bones are the ones in your wrists and ankles, and have less compact bone than long bones.

Flat bones are the ones in your skull and ribs. They are like bone sandwiches, with layers of compact bone on the outside and a layer of spongy bone in the middle.

Sesamoid bones are seed-shaped bones found inside muscles, like your kneecap, and irregular bones are all the other bones. They often have strange shapes, like your pelvis.

Each of your bones is a living tissue. Though they look like they don't do much, their cells are always busy keeping your skeleton strong.

BEHIND THE X-RAY

X-rays show doctors our bones. You might have even been to the hospital and seen your own! Use the space to draw what you're likely to see behind the X-ray…

FIVE THINGS YOU NEED TO KNOW ABOUT YOUR BONES

1 YOUR BONES BALANCE BLOOD
Bones can change the level of acid in your blood, helping to keep it steady.

2 YOU ALWAYS MAKE NEW BONE
Adults don't stop making bone, they replace ten percent of their skeleton each year.

3 SOME BONES BREAK OFTEN
The bones that people break most often are the ones in their arms!

4 ONE BONE ISN'T CONNECTED
The hyoid bone in your neck is the only bone that doesn't link to any others.

5 SOME JOINTS CAN'T MOVE
There are joints between the bones in your skull, but they don't move!

BONE PUZZLE

Place the bones in the right places to complete the puzzle.

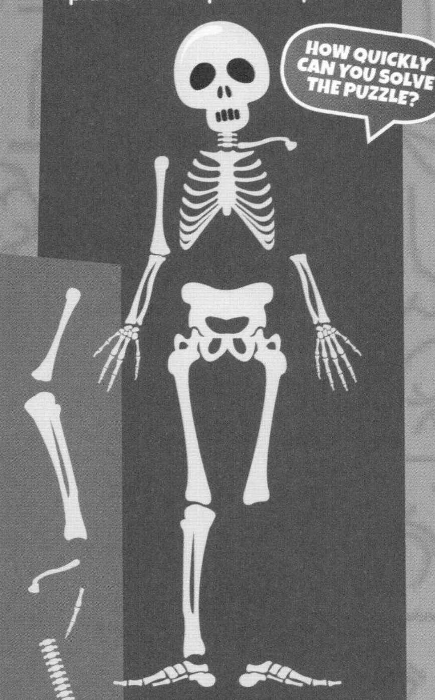

NERVES AND BLOOD VESSELS

MY MAIN JOB:

KEEPING THE BONE ALIVE

We run through the middle of the bone. We give bone cells fresh blood, and we send messages to and from the brain. We make sure the bone cells always have enough oxygen and nutrients, and we tell the brain if the bone gets hurt.

SPONGY BONE

HOW YOU PRONOUNCE MY NAME: spun-gee bone

MY MAIN JOB:

TO MAKE THE BONE LIGHT

If bones were solid all the way through, they would be really heavy! I have lots of holes that help to make bones lighter. I also help the ends of bones to cope when they get pushed from all directions.

COMPACT BONE

HOW YOU PRONOUNCE MY NAME: com-pakt bone

MY MAIN JOB:

TO MAKE THE BONE STRONG

I am the strong part of the bone. I am made from lots of layers of very hard bone tissue. It is my job to make sure that the bones don't break. I sometimes share my calcium with the rest of the body.

PERIOSTEUM

HOW YOU PRONOUNCE MY NAME: pe-ree-os-tee-yum

MY MAIN JOB:

COVERING THE BONE

I am the tissue that covers the outside of the bone. I help your bones to stay strong and healthy. If you break a bone, cells inside me will help to fix it.

MEDULLARY CAVITY

HOW YOU PRONOUNCE MY NAME: med-ul-a-ree kav-i-tee

MY MAIN JOB:

STORING BONE MARROW

I am a hole that runs right down the middle of the bone. People sometimes call me the marrow cavity. That's because I am the space that's full of bone marrow. Different bones contain different types of marrow.

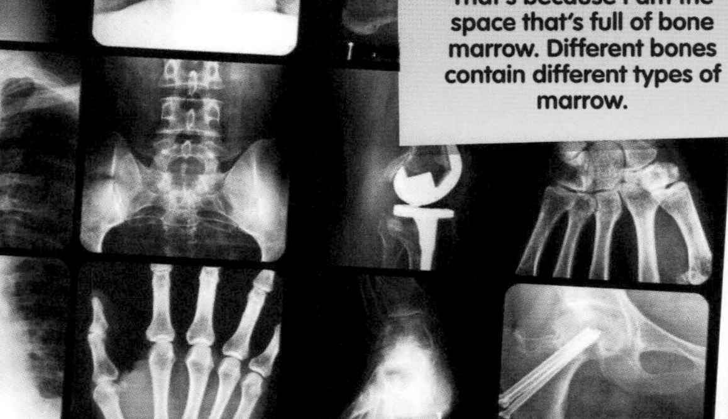

BONE MARROW

HOW YOU PRONOUNCE MY NAME: bone ma-row

MY MAIN JOB:

MAKING BLOOD CELLS

I am the soft tissue in the middle of the bone. I come in two types, red and yellow. Red marrow makes red and white blood cells. Yellow marrow contains fat cells, which store energy for the body.

© Getty Images

THE BONES IN YOUR BODY

Without your skeleton you would turn into a puddle of skin and organs on the floor! Your bones give you shape, they let you move, and they protect your brain, lungs, and heart. But that's not all.

Your bones are blood cell factories. If you looked inside them, you would find a special tissue called bone marrow. It makes two million new blood cells every single second!

They are also a calcium bank. Calcium makes your skeleton strong, but it also lets your heart beat and your nerves send messages. Your bones store calcium for the rest of your body so you never run out.

MANDIBLE

Some people call me the jawbone. I am actually one of the skull bones, but I'm not connected to the others. This means I can move on my own, letting you open and close your mouth.

CLAVICLE

Some people call me the collar bone. I link your rib cage to your shoulder. My job is to support your arm and shoulder blade, helping to keep them in the right place. I am one of the most fragile bones in the body.

STERNUM

Most people call me the breastbone. I am right in the middle of your chest. I connect to most of your ribs, forming the front of your rib cage. My job is to protect your heart and lungs.

PELVIS

I am the bowl-shaped bone at the bottom of your body – some call me the hip bone. My most important job is to support the muscles that help you walk. I also help to protect the soft organs inside your tummy.

PATELLA

Most people call me the kneecap, because I sit right in front of the knee joint. It's my job to keep your knee safe. I also help to move your legs. Your thigh muscles pull on me to straighten your knee.

BIG NUMBERS

206

WHEN YOU ARE FINISHED GROWING, YOU WILL HAVE 206 BONES IN YOUR BODY

20.5 POUNDS

YOUR SKELETON WEIGHS AROUND TWENTY-AND-A-HALF POUNDS

10

YOUR SKELETON COMPLETELY REPLACES ITSELF EVERY TEN YEARS

26

ONE IN EVERY 100 PEOPLE HAS TWENTY-SIX RIBS INSTEAD OF TWENTY-FOUR

4,000

YOUR THIGH BONE CAN TAKE 4,000 NEWTONS OF FORCE BEFORE IT BREAKS

106

YOUR HANDS AND FEET CONTAIN 106 BONES – MORE THAN HALF THE BONES IN YOUR BODY!

SKULL

I'm actually twenty-two different bones: eight around your brain, and fourteen in your face! Together, we keep your head safe. Your brain is your most important organ, and it's also one of the most fragile. We make sure it's well protected.

VERTEBRA

I am one of the bones in your spine – there are twenty-four of us all together! Having so many bones in your back means you can bend in all directions. We protect your spinal cord – the nerves that send messages from your brain to your body.

HUMERUS

You might have heard people call me the funny bone! I go from your shoulder to your elbow, where I make a joint with the bones in your forearm. My job is to help you lift and bend your arm.

RIB

I am a rib. There are twenty-four of us in your chest; twelve on each side. We make a cage around your heart and lungs to keep them safe. We also help your chest to move in and out so you can breathe.

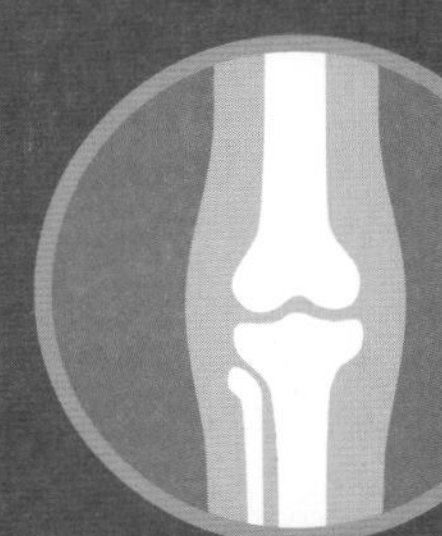

ULNA

I am the longest bone in your forearm. I connect your elbow to the outside of your wrist, by your little finger. My main job is to keep your arm and wrist steady when you pick things up and turn them over.

TIBIA

I am the big bone that runs down the front of your lower leg – some people call me the shin bone. I am the second biggest bone in the body! I connect your knee to your ankle, and like your femur, I carry your weight when you're standing, walking, and running.

FEMUR

I am the longest and strongest bone in the whole body! I go all the way from your hip to your knee. I need to be strong because I take all your weight all at once when you're running and hopping.

FIBULA

I am the smallest of the two bones in your lower leg. You can feel me on the outside edge of your ankle. I don't carry your weight; I just help to keep your ankle stable and support your muscles.

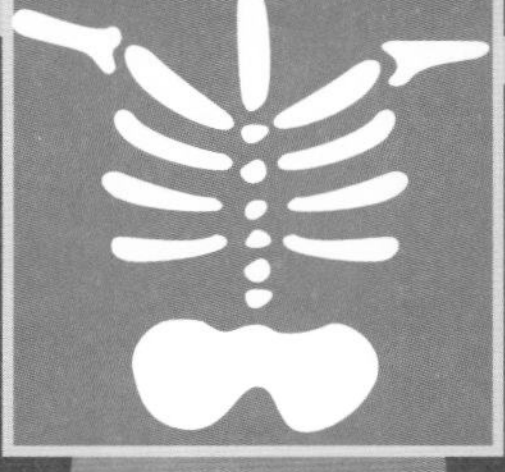

© Getty Images

IMMUNE SYSTEM: YOUR BODY DEFENDERS

Your immune system is a huge team of white blood cells that work together to keep you healthy. They defend your body against germs that try to make you sick.

There are two main types of germs that can get into your body: bacteria and viruses.

Bacteria are little cells, much smaller than the other cells in your body. They aren't all dangerous, but some make chemicals that can make you feel sick. Scientists call these chemicals toxins (pronounced toks-ins).

Viruses are even smaller than bacteria, and they aren't cells at all; they are just pieces of genetic code packed up into parcels. You might remember that genetic code tells your cells how to make proteins. If viruses get into your cells, they start telling your body to make virus proteins. That can make you feel sick.

Your immune system's job is to track these germs down and get rid of them.

Your immune system is made from white blood cells. They come from your bone marrow, and they move around your body in your blood. Just like soldiers in a real army, these cells are trained to do lots of different jobs.

Some of the cells guard your tissues. It's their job to spot the very first signs of an infection. These cells can eat bacteria, gobbling them up and stopping them from doing any damage. They also sound the alarm, telling other immune cells to come and help.

Some of these other cells make deadly chemicals that can kill bacteria, some of them kill cells that have been taken over by viruses, and some of them make little chemical missiles called antibodies. These stick to germs and trap them.

Once you've had a germ once, your immune system learns how to fight it faster. This means that you might not get sick if you catch the same germ again! This is called immunity.

IMMUNITY

IT REALLY IS AN ARMY

You have seven million white blood cells in every milliliter of your blood! They wait there in case a germ gets in. If they find an infection, they squeeze out of your blood and into your body to get rid of it.

YOU'RE MAKING MORE ALL THE TIME

Most white blood cells only live for around twenty-four hours. This means that you have to keep making new ones to make sure that you're protected against bacteria and viruses. Your body makes around 20,000 new white blood cells every single second.

IT REMEMBERS GERMS IT'S SEEN BEFORE

Your immune system has an incredible memory! Once it's fought a germ once, it learns how to fight it faster and better next time. But there's a catch: some germs, like flu, can change what they look like. This means your immune system has to learn to fight them all over again.

VACCINES

WHEN YOUR BODY NEEDS A BIT OF HELP

MMR VACCINE

I protect against three diseases: measles, mumps, and rubella. I am given to children when they are between one and three years old.

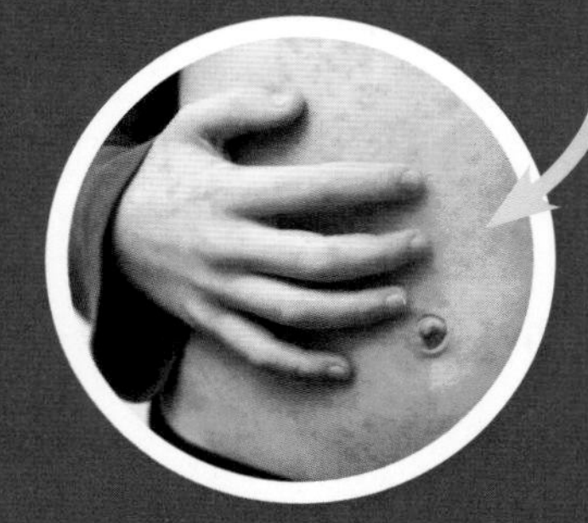

FLU VACCINE

I protect against seasonal flu, a virus that infects people's lungs in the winter. I am a spray that goes up your nose, and you need to have me every year.

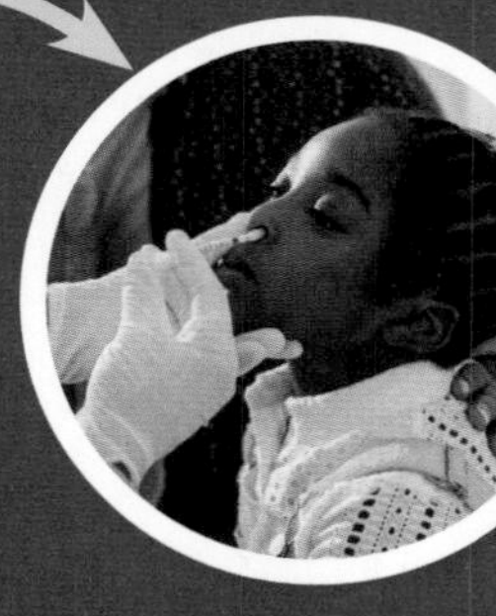

WORD SUDOKU

Played just like a regular sudoku, but with letters! Remember, you can only use I, M, M, U, N and E. Each of the six rows and columns, as well as each of the six subregions, must contain one, and only one, of each of the six letters.

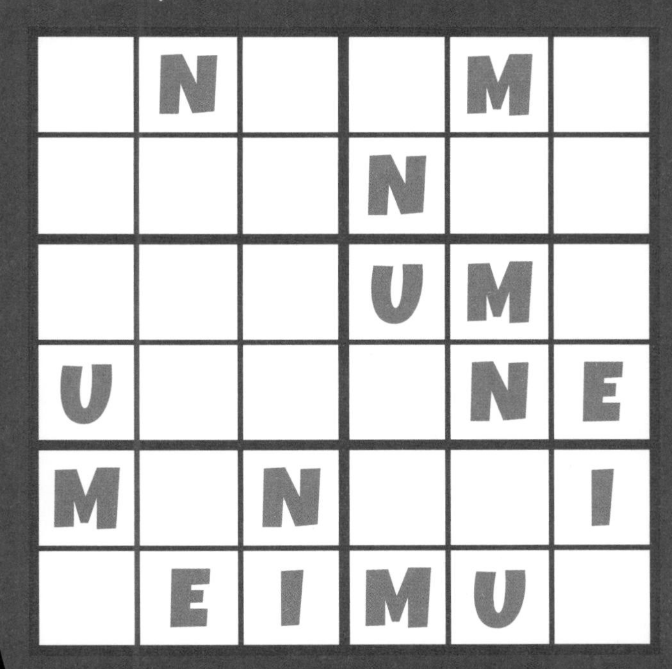

	N			M	
			N		
			U	M	
U				N	E
M		N			I
	E	I	M	U	

PNEUMOCOCCAL VACCINE

I protect against a type of bacteria that can cause meningitis. I am normally given to babies when they are twelve weeks old, and again when they are one year old.

ROTAVIRUS VACCINE

I protect against a virus that causes a bad stomachache. I am droplets that you swallow. Doctors normally give me to new babies in the first weeks after they're born.

HPV VACCINE

I protect against a virus that can cause cancer. I am given to children when they are around twelve years old.

COLOR IT IN!

A syringe has twenty-five centimeters of a vaccine. Color or mark on the picture how full it is.

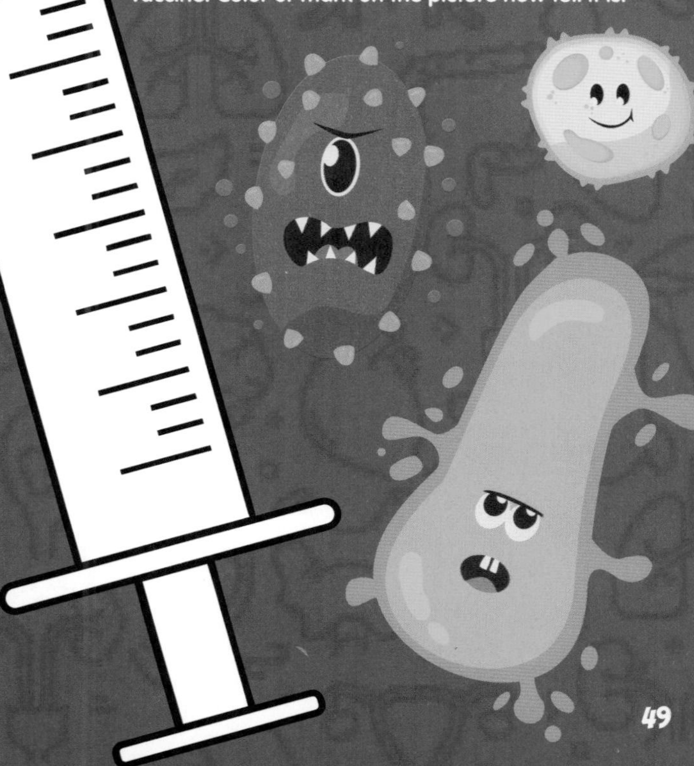

YOUR ORGANS: THE CELLS AND TISSUES THAT KEEP YOU ALIVE

Your organs are groups of cells and tissues that work together to do jobs inside your body. There are lots of jobs to do, so there are lots of different organs! You'll meet some of them in more detail elsewhere in this book. Here, we'll have a look at some of the most important.

Five of your organs are known as "vital organs." These are the ones you absolutely cannot live without. They are your brain, heart, kidneys, liver, and lungs.

These organs do essential jobs, like pumping blood around your body, making sure your cells have enough oxygen, and getting rid of toxic waste. You can survive with one kidney, or one lung, and you can even have part of your liver removed. But if you lost any of these organs completely, your body would just stop working.

Your other organs are important too, but doctors have found ways to help people live without them. They include your sense organs, like your eyes, ears, nose, and tongue, and your digestive organs, like your stomach and intestines.

Some of your organs, like your skin, are very big, but others are really quite small. You have an organ in your throat called your larynx (pronounced la-rinks). It contains your vocal cords, and its job is to let you talk.

Strangely, there is one organ that doesn't seem to do anything useful. Your appendix (pronounced a-pen-dicks) is a little organ connected to your large intestine. It's about two inches long, and it's the shape of a worm.

Scientists think that the appendix might be there to help the immune system fight infection, but lots of people have their appendix taken out, and their bodies don't seem to miss it at all!

ORGAN PUZZLE

Arrange the organs so that the same color or shape isn't in the same row horizontally, vertically, or diagonally. Draw them in pencil or on a notepad to make solving the puzzle easier.

WORD SEARCH

Now find each of your organs in the word search below.

I	X	H	J	D	E	N	B	R	A	I	N	X	I
F	O	N	K	F	S	U	Y	Q	N	X	H	J	N
J	H	H	S	K	I	N	H	I	A	D	S	W	T
P	D	I	X	Z	H	X	K	G	X	G	L	M	E
H	K	G	V	Q	C	F	L	X	S	G	Q	O	S
E	G	M	P	F	O	S	Y	X	T	Y	Z	W	T
A	D	A	K	A	T	X	J	R	O	I	N	F	I
R	L	M	L	I	V	E	R	F	M	X	G	X	N
T	O	H	U	L	G	Q	W	X	A	G	P	H	E
H	N	C	N	Y	T	P	X	D	C	F	J	Y	S
S	M	O	G	S	M	N	W	B	H	X	A	X	X
Q	K	T	S	I	L	M	L	I	H	F	C	G	H
U	E	K	E	S	T	J	G	L	D	S	T	N	I
Z	I	B	L	A	D	D	E	R	V	E	V	B	R

INTESTINES
BLADDER
LIVER
STOMACH
LUNGS
SKIN
HEART
BRAIN

YOUR ORGANS: THE CELLS AND TISSUES THAT KEEP YOU ALIVE

SKIN

HOW YOU PRONOUNCE MY NAME

skin

MY MAIN JOB:

PROTECTING YOU

I surround your entire body. It is my job to stop your insides from getting out, and to stop the outside from getting in! I am completely waterproof, and I contain colorful molecules that help to protect you from the sun.

BRAIN

brayn

MY MAIN JOB:

CONTROLLING YOUR BODY

I am the control center of your body. I send electrical signals through the nervous system to tell everything else what to do. I also listen for touch, taste, sight, smell, and sound signals from the body. I let you think, imagine, remember, plan, feel, and move.

LUNGS

HOW YOU PRONOUNCE MY NAME

lungs

MY MAIN JOB:

BREATHING

I am a set of stretchy bags in your chest. It is my job to get oxygen into your blood and take carbon dioxide out. Every breath you take moves around 500 milliliters of air into and out of me.

HEART

HOW YOU PRONOUNCE MY NAME

hart

MY MAIN JOB:

PUMPING BLOOD

I am one of the hardest-working muscles in your body. I beat around sixty times a minute, every minute of your life. Each beat sends blood around your body, carrying oxygen and nutrients to your cells and taking waste away.

LIVER

HOW YOU PRONOUNCE MY NAME

liv-er

MY MAIN JOB:

CLEANING BLOOD

I am one of your biggest organs! If you put your hands just under your ribs, you'll notice that your right side is warmer than your left. That's me! I clean chemicals out of your blood, make sure you have enough energy, and make bile to help you digest food.

STOMACH

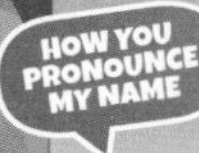

stum-ak

MY MAIN JOB:

DIGESTING FOOD

I am a stretchy bag just under your ribs. I collect all your food when you're eating, and squash it down into a paste before it moves on to your intestines. I am full of acid, which helps to kill any bacteria that might make you sick.

INTESTINES

HOW YOU PRONOUNCE MY NAME

in-tes-tins

MY MAIN JOB:

DIGESTING FOOD

I am the tube that connects your stomach to your bottom. All your food has to pass through me. It is my job to make sure that you get all the goodness out of your food. I take out all the nutrients and all the water, and get rid of the waste.

KIDNEY

kid-nee

MY MAIN JOB:

MAKING PEE

I am like a filter. It is my job to clean the waste out of your blood and turn it into pee. I make around a liter of pee every day, and I send it through long tubes to the bladder.

BLADDER

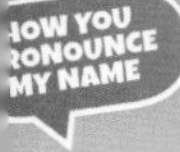

bla-dur

MY MAIN JOB:

STORING WEE

I am a stretchy bag at the very bottom of your tummy. I store wee until you're ready to go to the bathroom. Did you know that I can hold more wee at night than I can in the day?

© Getty Images

WHAT DO YOU KNOW ABOUT THE HUMAN BODY?

TEST YOURSELF!

Memorize the facts in this chapter, close the book, and write them down. How many can you remember and jot down in ten minutes?

Isn't your body amazing? You have so many different tissues and organs all working together to do different jobs.

You've met all the bones in your skeleton, from the longest and strongest, to the very smallest! You've followed the journey your food takes through your digestive system, all the way from your plate to the toilet bowl, and you've learned how your heart beats, day and night, to keep you and your cells alive.

You've looked inside your own eyes, learned how your ears respond to sounds, and found out how your muscles move your bones like pistons!

But the learning doesn't stop there. Your body is with you all the time, and you're a scientist in training, so it's time to start doing some experiments of your own. This book is packed with ideas to get you started. You could test your reflexes, take a hearing challenge, or even try to race your own heart.

Don't forget to take notes. Use the information you've learned here to make predictions about what you think might happen, and then test them for yourself. That's what real scientists do.

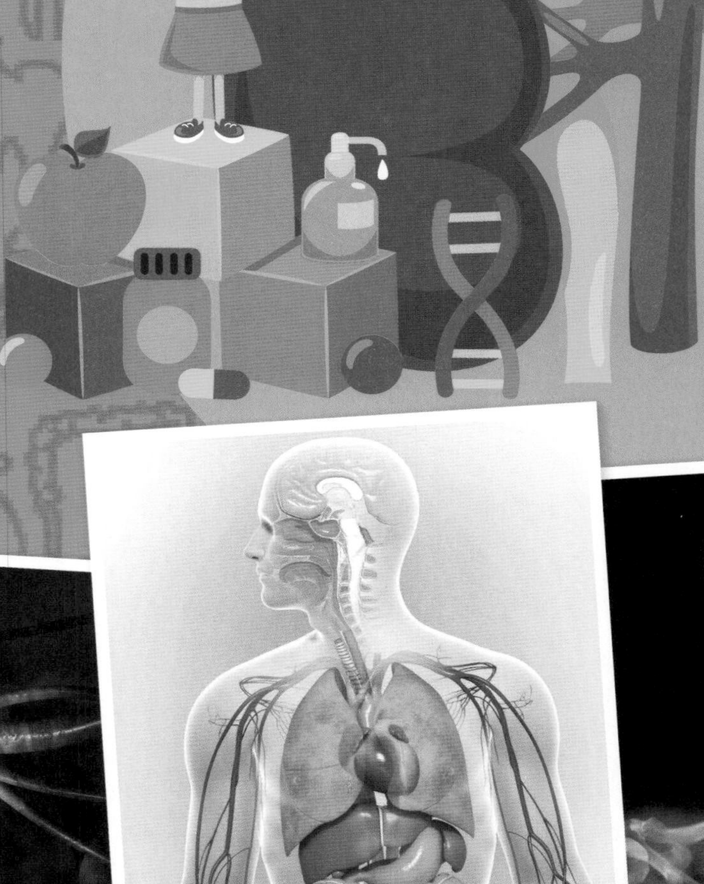

PUZZLE

Complete the puzzle of this colorful brain. Which piece doesn't fit?

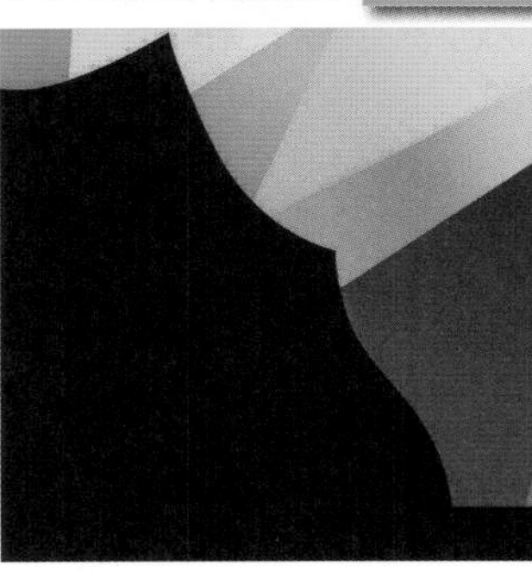

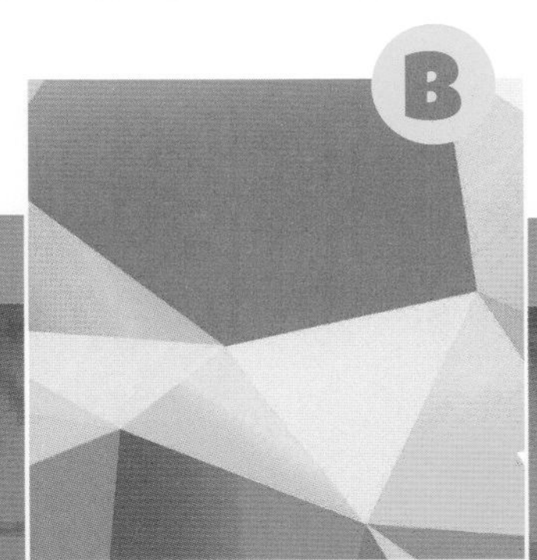

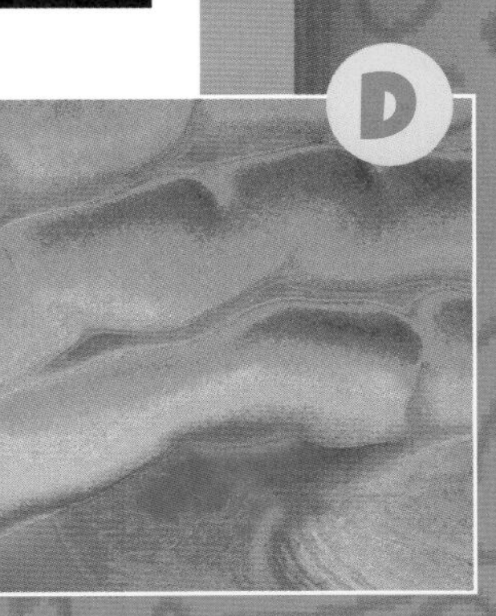

© Getty Images

HUMAN BODY PUZZLES

How quickly can you work out these puzzles about your body?

CROSSWORD

Below are the names of some things you met during the chapter, but can you fit them into the crossword?

HUMAN BODY
FUNNY BONE
NERVOUS SYSTEM
NOSE
EYES
FINGERS
HAIR
MUSCLES

SUDOKU

Fill in each of the squares with a number from 1 to 4. Remember, you're not allowed to repeat a number within a row, column or square. Hint: We've filled in some squares already.

	2	4	
1			3
4			2
	1	3	

HA! HA!

Make up some jokes with your friends about the human body. Which one is the funniest?

I SPY PUZZLE

Draw a line to link the body part to its correct function or characteristic

THIS CAN GET BURNED IN THE SUN	TEETH
YOU NEED THESE TO TEAR INTO FOOD	BRAIN
THIS IS HELPING YOU WORK OUT PUZZLES RIGHT NOW	SKIN
YOU USE THESE TO GIVE YOUR FRIENDS A HIGH FIVE!	EYES
THESE WILL HELP YOU RUN AND PLAY	HANDS
YOU NEED THESE TO READ AND SEE	LEGS

PLACE THE BODY PARTS

Place the body parts in the right part of the body. Can you slot them in in three minutes? How long does it take for you to place all of them?

LUNGS

BRAIN

LIVER

HEART

PANCREAS

STOMACH

KIDNEYS

SMALL INTESTINE

LARGE INTESTINE

© Getty Images

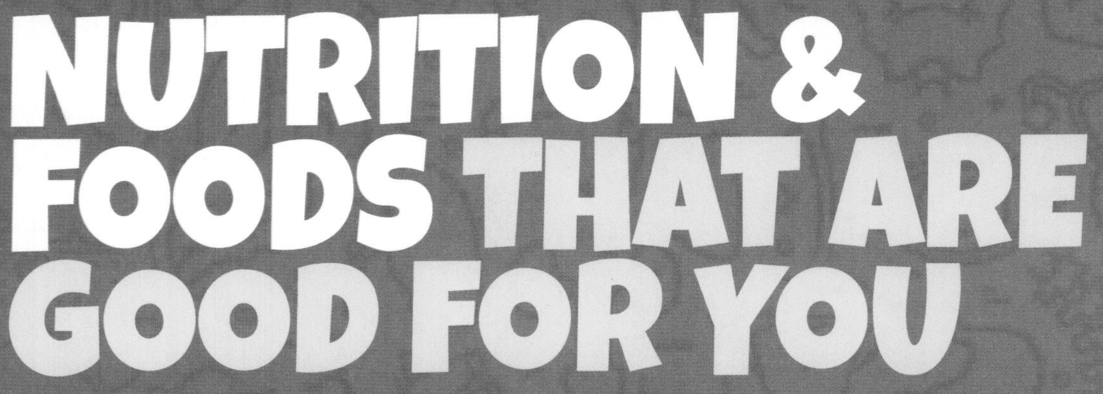

NUTRITION & FOODS THAT ARE GOOD FOR YOU

Your cells are always making new proteins, burning energy, and dividing to make new cells. So where do they get all the ingredients from? The answer is your food!

Everything you eat is made from molecules called proteins, carbohydrates, and fats. When you eat these molecules, your digestive system breaks them down into tiny blocks called amino acids, sugars, and fatty acids. Your cells then use these blocks to do all the building and repair work that they need to do inside your body.

They turn the amino acids into proteins, the sugars into energy, and the fatty acids into membranes and hormones.

Foods also contain nutrients called vitamins and minerals. Your cells use them for some of the most important jobs. Vitamin D and calcium make your bones strong. Sodium and potassium make your heart beat, and vitamin A helps you see in the dark.

Read on to find out more about how your food becomes your body, and how you can make sure you're giving your cells all the ingredients they need.

FRUIT SUMS

Fruit is a food that you will meet in this chapter. It is also very healthy and good for you. Can you work out the brainteaser below?

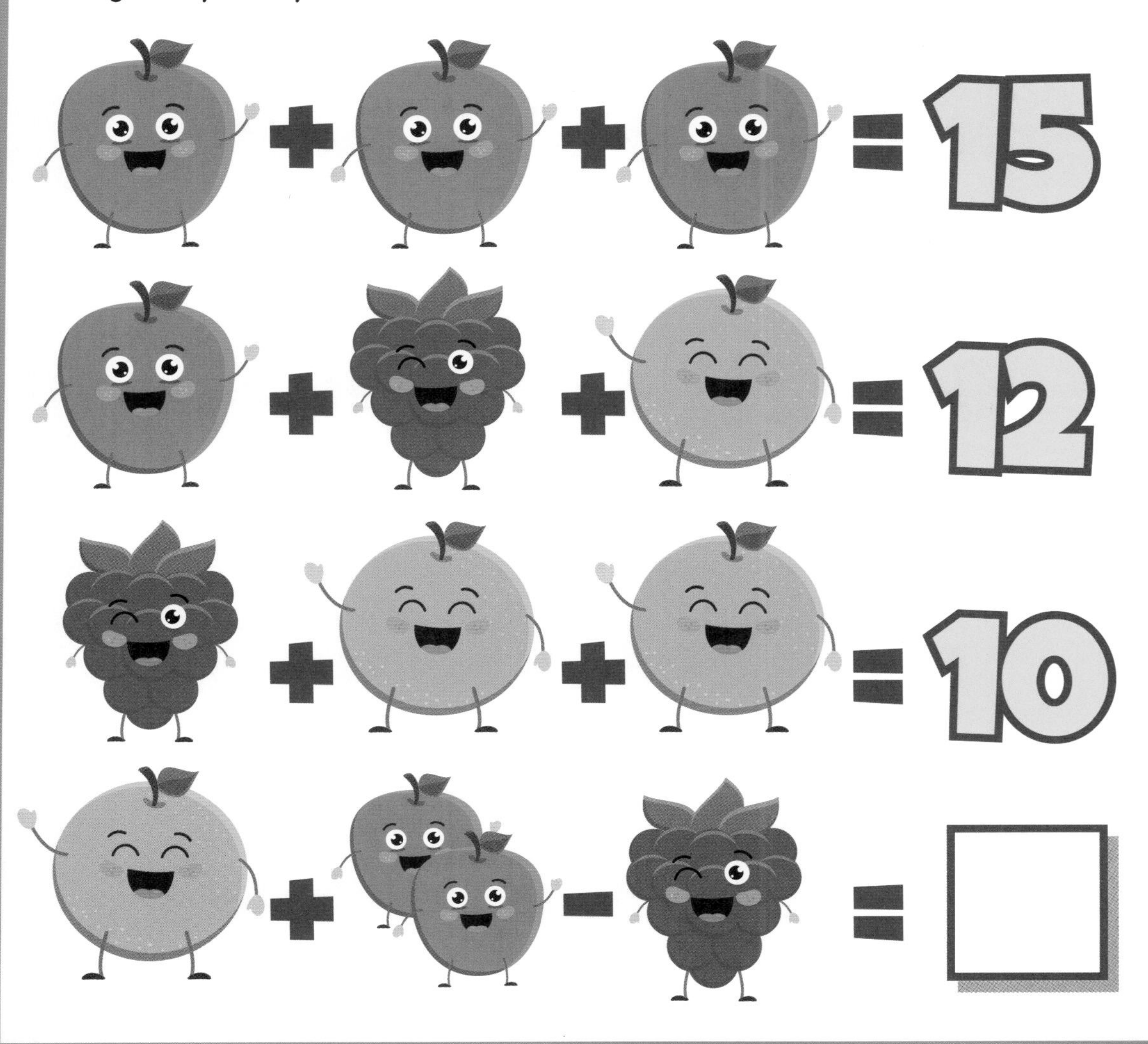

TRY IT OUT!

You will meet a mixture of foods in this chapter. Put either a sad face, happy face, or neutral face for foods that are bad for you, good for you, or that you can eat in moderation (you can eat it, but not too much of it!).

GOOD FOR YOU | EAT IN MODERATION | BAD FOR YOU

MUSHROOMS ☐ FRENCH FRIES ☐ OYSTERS ☐

PEANUT BUTTER ☐ BLUEBERRIES ☐ FISH ☐

COOKIES ☐ DARK CHOCOLATE ☐ LETTUCE ☐

© Getty Images

WHY IS NUTRITION SO IMPORTANT FOR ME?

Have you ever heard the phrase, "You are what you eat"? It's true! Your body breaks down the foods you eat and uses the pieces to build all your cells, tissues, and organs. That's why it's so important to eat good food.

There are two main things you need to get from your diet: macronutrients and micronutrients.

Macronutrients are the nutrients you need the most of (macro means big). They include proteins, carbohydrates, and fats. Your body uses these to build molecules and make energy.

Micronutrients are the nutrients you need small amounts of (micro means small). They include vitamins and minerals. Your body uses these to do important jobs, and it can't make them on its own.

Eating a balanced diet is about trying to get enough of these nutrients every day.

APPLE CHIPS

WHAT YOU'LL NEED

- 2 apples

INSTRUCTIONS

1. SLICE THE APPLES
Take the cores out of the apples and slice them very thinly to make lots of round shapes.
2. BAKE THE CHIPS
Lay the chips out on a baking sheet, and bake them for an hour at 280 degrees Fahrenheit.
3. CHECK AND TURN
Part way through the bake, take the chips out of the oven and turn them over.
4. SAVE SOME FOR LATER!
When the apples are done, they should be dry and golden. You can store them in an airtight container.

RAINBOW TORTILLA PIZZA

WHAT YOU'LL NEED

- Muffin tray
- Round cookie cutter
- Flour tortillas
- Tomato puree
- Grated cheese
- Rainbow vegetables

INSTRUCTIONS

1. CUT THE PIZZA BASES
Use the cookie cutter to cut twelve round shapes from your flour tortillas.
2. PREPARE THE TIN
Grease the muffin tin and press one of the cut tortillas in each hole to form a little case.
3. ADD TOMATO AND CHEESE
Put a spoonful of tomato paste in each case, and sprinkle with grated cheese.
4. ADD THE RAINBOW!
Add chopped vegetables to each case. Can you find one of every color of the rainbow?
5. BAKE IN THE OVEN
Bake your rainbow tortilla pizzas in the oven for ten minutes at 390 degrees Fahrenheit until they are golden.

TWO-INGREDIENT BANANA PANCAKES

WHAT YOU'LL NEED

- 2 bananas
- 2 eggs

INSTRUCTIONS

1 MASH THE BANANAS
Using the back of a fork, mash the bananas until all the big lumps are gone.

2 MIX IN THE EGGS
Crack the eggs into the mashed banana and whisk them together with a fork.

3 START FRYING
Warm a little oil in a frying pan over a medium heat. Spoon the batter into the pan to make small pancakes.

4 FLIP THE PANCAKES!
After about a minute, you should start to see bubbles forming. Flip the pancakes over and cook the other side.

FRESH FRUIT POPSICLES

WHAT YOU'LL NEED

- Popsicle mold
- Fruit juice
- Fresh fruit

INSTRUCTIONS

1 PREPARE THE MOLDS
Pour about two centimeters of fruit juice into each popsicle mold, and put them into the freezer until they're solid.

2 PREPARE YOUR FRUIT
While you're waiting for the juice to freeze, choose some fruits and cut them into bite-sized pieces.

3 MAKE THE POPSICLES
Take the molds out of the freezer and half fill them with fruit pieces. Add a popsicle stick and fill up with juice.

4 FREEZE AND ENJOY
Put the popsicles back in the freezer for a few hours until they are completely frozen.

© Getty Images

VITAMINS: NUTRIENTS THAT KEEP YOU ALIVE

You probably know that fruits and vegetables are good for you because they contain vitamins. But what are vitamins, and why are they so important anyway?

Vitamins are nutrients that your body needs, but can't make on its own. The only way you can get them is to eat them.

While you're growing, vitamins help your body to make new skin, bones, and muscles. When you're an adult, they help your body to keep those tissues working and fix them when they break. If you don't get enough vitamins then your body won't be able to do these jobs.

Take vitamin C, for example. You find it in citrus fruits like oranges, lemons, and limes. Your body uses it to make a molecule called collagen (pronounced col-ah-jen).

Collagen comes in long strings that work a bit like glue. That glue holds your skin cells together. Without collagen, you start to fall apart! That's what used to happen to sailors and pirates.

It was hard to keep fruit and vegetables fresh on long sea voyages, so sailors used to survive on salted meat, biscuits, and rum. This meant that they didn't get enough vitamin C, and their bodies stopped making the glue that held their cells together.

This caused a disease called scurvy. Their teeth fell out, and their ribs started to rattle when they moved.

Around 300 years ago, doctors finally worked out what was wrong, and sailors started to drink lime juice on long voyages. This gave their bodies the vitamin C they needed and stopped them from getting sick.

That's why it's so important to eat fruits and vegetables. They might not be as tasty as chocolate and burgers, but they give your body nutrients that it can't get anywhere else.

VITAMIN E

This vitamin is important for healthy skin and eyes. It also supports your immune system and helps your nerve cells to send messages.

VITAMIN C

This vitamin helps your body to make the glue that holds your cells together. It's really important for healthy skin and gums.

VITAMIN A

This vitamin helps you to see! It also helps your immune system to fight infections, and keeps your lungs, kidneys, and heart healthy.

VITAMIN B

There are lots of different B vitamins! They help your body to do all kinds of things, from making new DNA to releasing energy from your food.

VITAMIN D

Your body makes this vitamin from sunlight! Its most important job is to help your bones grow strong and straight.

TASTY NUMBERS

5 Eat five portions of fruit and vegetables a day for vitamins A, C, and K

2 Eat oily fish twice a week for a boost of vitamin D and omega 3

1 Drink a glass of milk every day to get enough calcium for your bones

4 Eat four servings of whole grains a day to get a vitamin B boost

CARROTS

WHICH VITAMIN I CONTAIN:

A

Have you ever heard that carrots help you see in the dark? It's true! They contain a chemical called beta carotene – it's what makes them orange. Your body turns beta carotene into vitamin A, and uses it to look after your eyes.

PEAS

WHICH VITAMIN I CONTAIN:

B1

Peas are jam-packed with vitamin B1, sometimes called riboflavin (pronounced ri-bo-flay-vin). You need this vitamin to get the energy out of your food and keep your nervous system healthy. You can also find it in bananas, nuts, and wholegrain bread.

ORANGE

WHICH VITAMIN I CONTAIN:

C

Oranges and other citrus fruits like lemons and limes are full of vitamin C – so full, in fact, that you only need one orange to get all the vitamin C you need for the day! If you don't like oranges, you can get vitamin C from red peppers, broccoli, strawberries, pineapples, and kiwis.

BROCCOLI

WHICH VITAMIN I CONTAIN:

K

This tree-shaped vegetable is full of vitamins, but one of the most important is vitamin K. It helps your body to stop bleeding when you cut yourself. It also keeps your bones healthy and helps wounds to heal. You can find it in other green vegetables too, like spinach.

NUTS AND SEEDS

WHICH VITAMIN I CONTAIN:

E

Do you have a favorite nut? It's probably packed with vitamin E. This vitamin is essential for healthy skin. Try having nut butter on your toast in the morning, eating a handful of nuts after school, or adding nuts to cookies when you're baking. If you're allergic to nuts, don't worry – you can get vitamin E from seeds too.

TALK IT OUT!

Have a discussion with your friends on what kinds of foods contain vitamins. When did you last eat them?

FOOD DIARY

Keep a log over the next few weeks of how many vitamins you consume. Are you eating the right amount on a weekly basis?

	MONDAY	TUESDAY	WEDNESDAY	THURSDAY	FRIDAY	SATURDAY	SUNDAY
BREAKFAST							
LUNCH							
DINNER							
SNACKS							

© Getty Images

CARBOHYDRATES: EAT THESE FOR ENERGY!

Carbohydrates, also known as carbs, are the main way you get your energy, and they also help to keep your digestive system healthy. Did you know that most of them are made by plants? Even the white sugar you use to make cakes!

Plants make three main kinds of carbohydrates: sugars, starches, and fiber. Sugars are the simplest type of carbohydrate. Your body can use them for energy just as they are. When you eat sugary foods, your intestines pass the sugars straight into your blood. If your cells need energy right away, they pick the sugar up and start using it. But if they don't, your body stores it for later. It does this by releasing a hormone called insulin.

Insulin tells your liver, fat cells, and muscles to take the extra sugar out of your blood. Your liver and muscles stick the sugar together into chains and pack it away for later. Your fat cells turn it into fat.

Your body can get energy out of these stores whenever it needs to, helping to make sure your cells never run out of fuel.

The next type of carbohydrate made by plants is starch. Starch is just a chain of sugar molecules joined together one after the other. It doesn't taste as sweet as sugar, but it still has lots of energy that your body can use.

When you eat starchy foods like bread, pasta, or rice, your digestive system has to break the chains apart to release the sugar molecules. Once it has done that, those sugar molecules get into the blood, just like before, and insulin clears them away.

The last type of carbohydrate made by plants is fiber. Like starch, it's made from long chains of sugar, but this time your body can't break it down. This means it just passes straight through your system.

So what's the point of eating fiber? Well, because fiber doesn't break down, it keeps everything moving through your intestines. It also holds on to water, which helps to keep your poo soft and easy to pass.

FRUIT

WHICH CARB I CONTAIN:

SUGAR

If you're looking for a quick energy boost, fruits are a good choice! They taste sweet because they're packed with sugars, the easiest type of carbohydrates for your body to pick up and use straight away. Fruit contains two types of sugar: fructose (pronounced frook-toes), and glucose (pronounced gloo-koze). They get into your blood, sending energy to all your cells.

OATS

WHICH CARB I CONTAIN:

SOLUBLE FIBER

There are two main types of fiber in your food. Soluble fiber is fiber that dissolves in water. When you eat it, it makes a kind of gel in your digestive system. This gel helps to keep the bacteria in your large intestine happy, and they help to keep your body healthy.

VEGETABLES

WHICH CARB I CONTAIN:

INSOLUBLE FIBER

The other type of fiber in your food is insoluble fiber. This type of fiber does not dissolve in water, but it does attract water. Your body can't break it down, so it travels through your digestive system whole, taking water with it. This helps to keep your poo soft.

CARB TYPES

SUGAR

This type of carbohydrate gives your body instant energy! Your cells can use sugar molecules to recharge their chemical batteries.

STARCH

This type of carbohydrate gives you all-day energy. Starch is made from sugar, but it takes your body a while to get the sugar out, making the energy last longer.

FIBER

This type of carbohydrate keeps your digestive system moving. Your body can't break it down, so it travels all the way through and comes out the other end.

RICE, PASTA, AND BREAD

WHICH CARB I CONTAIN:

STARCH

For energy that lasts a bit longer, choose foods that contain starch. Your body can break starch down into sugars, but it takes a little while. This gives you a steadier supply of energy than eating sugary foods like fruit. Starchy foods include rice, pasta, bread, and potatoes.

MAZE

Carbohydrates also help the brain to function. A single slice of bread contains about six grams of carbohydrates. How quickly can you complete the maze?

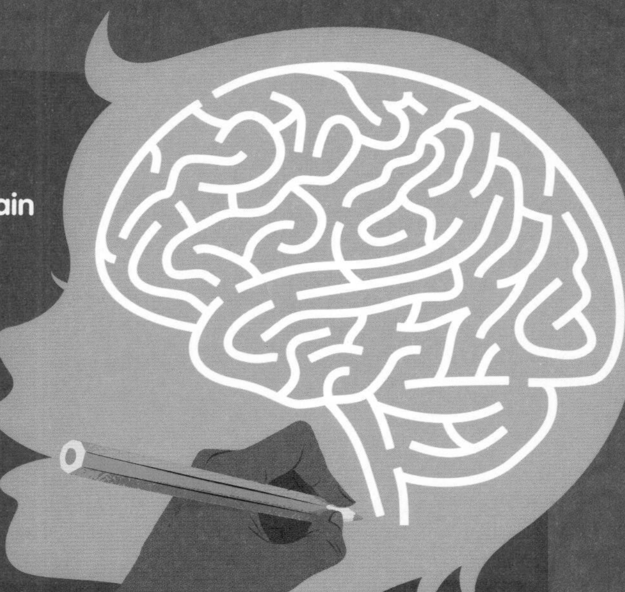

FOOD DIARY

Keep a log over the next few weeks of how many carbohydrates you consume. Are you eating the right amount on a weekly basis?

	MONDAY	TUESDAY	WEDNESDAY	THURSDAY	FRIDAY	SATURDAY	SUNDAY
BREAKFAST							
LUNCH							
DINNER							
SNACKS							

BIG NUMBERS

24 GRAMS

Try not to eat more than six teaspoons of sugar in a day

50%

Try to get half of your calories from starchy foods like pasta, rice, and potatoes

30 GRAMS

Eat thirty grams (one ounce) of fiber every day to keep your digestive system moving

25%

Around a quarter of your fiber should be soluble (try oats, fruits, and beans)

© Getty Images

FATS: THE FOOD THAT ALL YOUR CELLS ARE MADE OF

Your body needs fat to survive! It's one of the most important things you can eat. But it has a bad reputation.

If humans eat more food than they need, their bodies turn the extra energy into fat. This fat gets stored under the skin and around the organs, and it can sometimes make people ill. But that does not mean that eating fat is always bad; your body stores fat because it's useful!

Fat is a really important source of energy. People aren't always lucky enough to eat dinner every day. If they miss a meal, it's useful to have some spare energy inside their bodies to keep them going.

A little bit of fat under your skin is also really helpful when it's cold, because it works a bit like a blanket!

Eating fat does some other useful things for your body too. Do you remember what the membranes around your cells are made of? Fats! Every cell in your body is surrounded by a bubble of fat.

There is so much fat around your nerve cells that if you measured it all out, you'd discover that your brain is sixty percent fat!

Some hormones are made of fats too. These chemicals pass messages around your body, and if you didn't eat any fat, you wouldn't be able to make them.

You'll find different kinds of fat in your food, and some of them are healthier than others. Unsaturated fats, found in fish, nuts, and seeds, are better for your body than saturated fats, which are found in meat, eggs, and dairy products.

Eating healthy fats helps you to get the vitamins you need. Vitamins A, D, E, and K are called "fat soluble" (pronounced sol-you-bull) vitamins because they dissolve in fats. This means that fats help to carry them into your body.

LIPIDS

SATURATED FATS

These fats are a good source of energy. It's important not to eat too much of them because they can harm your heart.

UNSATURATED FATS

These fats give you energy, help to build and repair your cells, and keep your heart healthy.

OILY FISH

WHICH FATS I CONTAIN:

OMEGA THREE

I am one of the best foods to eat for omega three fats. These are a special kind of unsaturated fat that your body needs to keep your heart and brain healthy. Try eating two portions of oily fish every week to make sure that you get enough.

BUTTER

WHICH FATS I CONTAIN:

SATURATED FAT

Like lots of the fats that come from animals, I am solid at room temperature. That's how you can tell that I'm a saturated fat. I'm good for energy, but I'm not as healthy as foods that contain unsaturated fats, so eat me in moderation.

BIG NUMBERS

35%

You can get up to thirty-five percent of your daily energy from fat

30G

Men should try not to eat more than thirty grams (one ounce) of saturated fat a day

20 GRAMS

Women should try not to eat more than twenty grams of saturated fat a day

2X

Fat contains twice as much energy per gram as sugar!

PROCESSED FOODS

WHICH FATS I CONTAIN:

TRANS FAT

Processed foods like me can contain high levels of a bad type of fat called trans fat. Eating too many of these fats can make you more likely to have problems with your heart when you're older. It is a good idea to eat less of me and more unsaturated fat.

NUT BUTTER

WHICH FATS I CONTAIN:

UNSATURATED FAT

Nuts like me contain heart healthy unsaturated fats. We are still high in energy, but we are also good for your heart, skin, and brain. If you have a nut allergy, you can find unsaturated fats in other foods, like seeds, fish, and avocado.

SORT THE FATS

Some of the fats are in the wrong categories. Which should sit under unsaturated and which should be under saturated?

SATURATED

UNSATURATED

FOOD DIARY

Keep a log over the next few weeks of how many fats you consume. Are you eating the right amount on a weekly basis?

	MONDAY	TUESDAY	WEDNESDAY	THURSDAY	FRIDAY	SATURDAY	SUNDAY
BREAKFAST							
LUNCH							
DINNER							
SNACKS							

© Getty Images

GOOD FOOD VS BAD FOOD

No foods are completely good or completely bad, but there are some foods that are better for your body than others. The secret to staying healthy is to eat a mixture of different things. That way, you'll give your body all the nutrients it needs.

There are six different groups of foods that you should always try to include in your healthy diet.

Group one is fruit and vegetables, which are full of vitamins and fiber. They help to keep your cells healthy, and your digestive system moving. Try to eat five different kinds every day!

Group two is starchy foods like potatoes, bread, rice, and pasta. These are the foods that give you most of your energy. Choose one of these for every meal.

Group three is dairy products (or dairy alternatives if you're vegetarian, vegan, or dairy-free). These include foods like cows" milk, soy milk, yogurt, and cheese. They contain the mineral calcium, which is essential for building healthy bones.

Group four is protein, which includes meat, fish, eggs, beans, and lentils. These foods are important for building and repairing your body.

Group five is fat. Sometimes you will hear people say that fat is bad for you, but that isn't true! Your body needs fat to make the membranes around your cells and to keep your brain healthy. The trick is to choose mostly unsaturated fats, like oily fish, nuts, and avocados.

Finally, group six is water. Your body is half water, so you need to make sure that you drink enough throughout the day.

Don't forget to have treats sometimes too. Cakes, biscuits, chocolate, sweets, and chips might not be super healthy, but they can form part of a balanced diet. However, these foods are high in sugar and fat, so try not to eat them too often!

SWEET POTATO

WHY I'M GOOD FOR YOU:

See my orange color? Your body turns that into vitamin A.

APPLES

WHY I'M GOOD FOR YOU:

I have lots of fiber to keep your digestive system moving.

EAT IN MODERATION

CHEESE

WHY I SHOULD BE EATEN IN MODERATION:

I contain calcium and protein, but I've also got quite a lot of fat.

CHOCOLATE

WHY I SHOULD BE EATEN IN MODERATION:

Cocoa helps your heart, but I can contain a lot of sugar.

EAT LESS OF

SWEETS

WHY I SHOULD EAT LESS OF ME:

I don't have any vitamins, minerals, protein, or fiber.

SOFT DRINKS

WHY I SHOULD EAT LESS OF ME:

I can contain up to nine teaspoons of sugar per can!

YOGURT

WHY I'M GOOD FOR YOU:

I contain calcium, which helps your bones to grow strong.

SEAWEED

WHY I'M GOOD FOR YOU:

I am full of minerals like calcium, magnesium, and iron.

EGG

WHY I'M GOOD FOR YOU:

I am stuffed with vitamins, protein, and healthy fats.

RED MEAT

WHY I SHOULD BE EATEN IN MODERATION:

I am packed with protein, but too much of me can hurt your heart.

CAKE

WHY I SHOULD BE EATEN IN MODERATION:

Treats like me often don't have much fiber or vitamins.

FRUIT JUICE

WHY I SHOULD BE EATEN IN MODERATION:

I am one of your five a day, but I contain quite a lot of sugar.

CHIPS

WHY I SHOULD EAT LESS OF ME:

I am high in fat and salt, and low in fiber and vitamins.

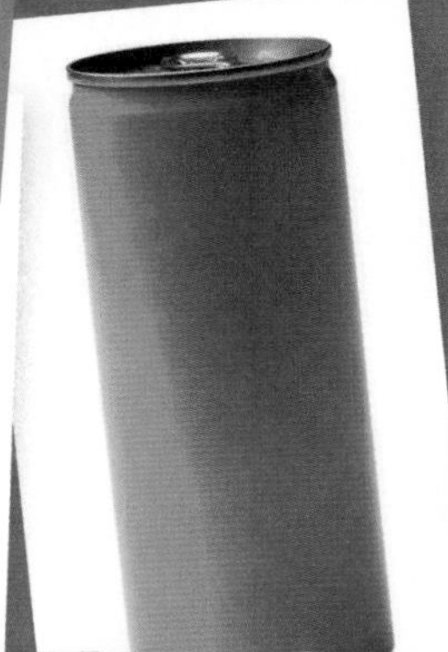

ENERGY DRINKS

WHY I SHOULD EAT LESS OF ME:

I can contain up to nine teaspoons of sugar per can!

CROSSWORD

Slot the names of the good foods on this page into this crossword. Unscramble the colored squares to reveal another food. Is it healthy or unhealthy?

ANSWER: Toast

TRY IT OUT!

Decide with your friends what would make a healthy meal and unhealthy meal. What would be in it?

© Getty Images

END OF NUTRITION

Your whole body is built from the foods that you put in your mouth. Every time you eat something, you are sending fresh ingredients to your cells. They use those ingredients to make and mend your tissues. The dinner you eat this evening will be red blood cells by this time next week!

That's why it's so important to eat a healthy diet. The foods you choose have a big impact on how healthy your body is.

The most important thing to remember is to give your body variety. It needs lots of different nutrients to stay healthy. Mixing up the foods you put on your plate is the best way to give your body everything it needs.

Eating a rainbow of fruits and vegetables will help to make sure that you get all the vitamins your body wants. Making sure you have protein, carbohydrates, and fat on your plate will make sure that your body has the building blocks it needs to make new molecules and to keep your chemical batteries charged. Eating a little of the foods you really enjoy, even if they're not that healthy, will make you happy. That's a really important part of a balanced diet too!

TEST YOURSELF! 3

Memorize the facts, close the book, and write them down. How many can you jot down in three minutes?

WATCH THIS!

FACTS ABOUT NUTRITION

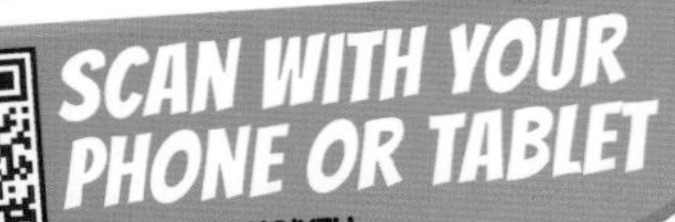

FATS, OILS, & SWEETS

MEAT, FISH, & EGGS

DAIRY

FRUITS & VEGETABLES

BREAD, CEREALS, & GRAINS

DRAW IT!

Using the spaces provided, draw a picture of the foods that are listed in the triangle. Which is your favorite food and when did you last eat it?

CRACK THE CODE!

Match the food items to the letters to complete the sentence below. What does it tell you to do?

I should eat ☐☐☐☐ portions of fruit and

☐☐☐☐☐☐☐☐☐☐ a day

© Getty Images

ANSWERS: FIVE, VEGETABLES

NUTRITION PUZZLES

How much do you know about what's good for your body?

DRAW A BALANCED MEAL

Discuss with your friends what would make a healthy, balanced meal. Draw a picture on the plate provided.

SUDOKU

Fill in each of the squares with each of the foods. Remember, you're not allowed to repeat an image within a row, column, or square. Hint: We've filled in some squares already.

COLOR IT IN

Color the image in and decide which of the foods has fats, vitamins, proteins, or carbohydrates. Then work out which foods are healthy and unhealthy.

TRY IT OUT!

Below are three buckets: proteins, fats, and vitamins. Read through the chapter again, and then place each of the food types that contain fats, vitamins, and proteins into the right bucket.

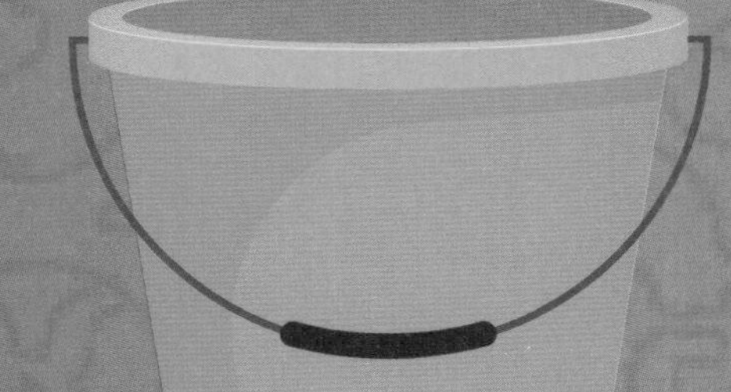

© Getty Images

YOUR GENETICS

Genes are one of the most important discoveries in the history of science! They contain the instructions to make the human body, and they pass down from one generation to the next. The science of genetics helps us to understand how genes work, and where they came from.

Genes are a part of your genetic code. They are written on a molecule called DNA. It's like a chemical book, full of letters that spell out how to build your body – and it's enormous!

If you wanted to store all the letters of your DNA on a computer, it would take up three gigabytes of memory!

Amazingly, each of your cells stores its own copy of the genetic code. If you stretched out the strands of DNA from one cell, they would be taller than the average person! The genes inside tell your cells how to make proteins, the machines that make your body live, repair, and grow.

In this chapter, you'll find out where your genes came from, how they work, and how your body keeps them safe. You'll learn about DNA and chromosomes, and you'll have a chance to do some experiments to understand genetics for yourself.

YOUR GENES

Circle the parts of the body that are influenced by your genes before reading this chapter. Which parts of you did you inherit from your parents?

WATCH THIS!

WHAT ARE TRAITS?

SCAN WITH YOUR PHONE OR TABLET

https://bit.ly/3CvWK7b

© Getty Images

WHAT EXACTLY ARE GENES?

Genes are one of the most important parts of your body. You started out as a single cell and grew into a whole human being, all because your cells followed the instructions in your genes.

So how many genes do you think it took to build your body? The answer is around 25,000. That really surprised scientists when they first found out. They thought it would take many, many more. Those genes work together to do everything from growing your hair to thinking.

Genes are also the engines of evolution. They are how living things pass instructions from one generation to the next. They change very slightly each time they pass on, and over millions of years, those tiny changes add up to big differences.

Every plant and animal on the planet evolved from the same prehistoric ancestor, so we all still share some of our genes. Take a look at the graphic on this page to see what percentage of your genes you share with other animals.

In this chapter, you will take a dive into your genetics. You'll discover the secrets of DNA, unlock your chromosomes, and find out how you got your genes in the first place.

FIVE THINGS YOU NEED TO KNOW ABOUT YOUR GENETICS

1 ONLY 1% OF YOUR DNA IS GENES
The rest tells your cells when to turn those genes on or off.

2 YOU HAVE TWO COPIES OF EACH GENE
You get one copy from each of your biological parents.

3 SOME GENES ARE VERY LONG
Your longest gene has more than two million letters of instructions.

4 OTHER GENES ARE VERY SHORT
Your shortest gene has only 800 letters of instructions.

5 MOST GENES ARE IN THE MIDDLE
Most of your genes are around 50,000 letters long.

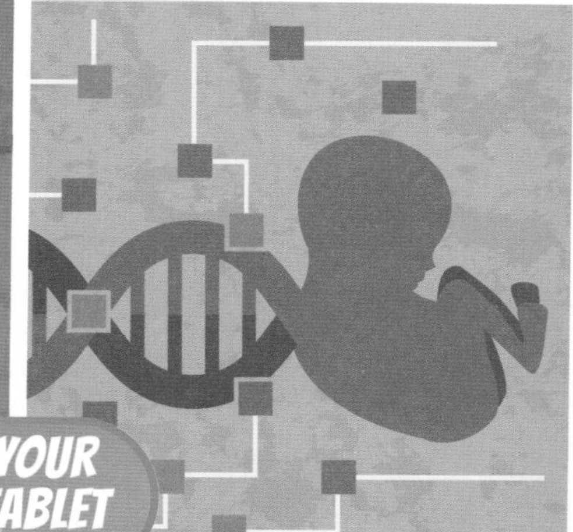

WATCH THIS!
WHAT ARE GENES?

SCAN WITH YOUR PHONE OR TABLET
https://bit.ly/3BZs4uw

WHO DO I SHARE MY GENETICS WITH?

99%
OUR CLOSEST RELATIVES ARE
CHIMPANZEES
WE SHARE A LOT OF THE SAME GENES

85%
MICE
ARE MAMMALS JUST LIKE US, SO WE SHARE A LOT OF GENES

60%

CHICKENS ARE MORE CLOSELY RELATED TO DINOSAURS THAN THEY ARE TO US

40%

WE MIGHT LOOK VERY DIFFERENT, BUT WE STILL SHARE SOME GENES WITH **WORMS**

COLOR IN THE PERCENTAGES

Now that you know the proportions, color in the circles to match the percentages

© Getty Images, Alamy

YOUR CHROMOSOMES: THE X-SHAPES THAT MAKE YOU, YOU

You have so much DNA inside each of your cells – six whole feet. Left to its own devices, that much DNA could get really untidy really quickly, so your cells pack it up into forty-six little parcels called chromosomes.

Each chromosome is a single thread of DNA wrapped around thousands of tiny proteins called histones (pronounced hiss-tohn). These proteins look a bit like the spools that keep thread tidy on a sewing machine. Histones keep your DNA wrapped up neatly until your cells need to use it.

To use a gene, all a cell needs to do is unwind the histone and let the DNA out.

If you looked at your chromosomes under a microscope, you would notice a few interesting things. First, they're brightly colored! The word chromosome literally means "colorful body" in ancient Greek. This is because chromosomes suck up the purple dye scientists use to make cells show up under the microscope.

The second thing you would notice is that your chromosomes come in pairs – twenty-three pairs, to be exact. You got one set from each of your biological parents, giving you two copies of every gene.

The third thing you would notice is that most of the time, your chromosomes are sausage shaped. But before a cell divides, they become X-shaped! This is because the cell has copied all of the DNA and made a brand new chromosome. That new one stays attached to the old one until the cell splits and pulls the two copies apart.

The last thing you would notice is that one pair of chromosomes is a bit different from the rest. Scientists call these the sex chromosomes. Their job is to decide your biological sex, whether you are genetically male or female. In genetic females, the sex chromosomes both look like X-shapes, but, in genetic males, one of the sex chromosomes looks like a Y-shape!

WORD SEARCH

How many of the words can you find in the word search below?

LONG ARM · CENTROMERE · ARM · CHROMOSOME · DNA · PROTEINS · SHORT · HISTONES

L	T	A	V	L	M	P	K	P	G	D	B	C	I
O	O	X	O	P	X	H	T	L	D	N	X	H	T
N	F	R	N	J	R	G	K	Q	H	X	R	R	H
G	X	P	A	Z	X	O	X	X	D	N	A	O	K
A	R	M	M	P	T	G	T	G	H	E	R	M	W
R	V	J	M	C	R	H	Q	E	X	J	K	O	J
M	E	P	G	W	O	D	F	J	I	A	J	S	G
X	N	G	S	Y	H	I	H	Q	Z	N	X	O	F
H	R	M	H	H	S	Y	L	H	X	H	S	M	M
B	M	A	G	H	O	F	X	K	G	D	C	E	N
O	E	H	I	S	T	O	N	E	S	K	X	D	X
P	T	L	I	K	M	Q	S	T	K	I	K	H	G
K	M	K	U	J	L	R	X	U	Z	G	L	R	J
C	E	N	T	R	O	M	E	R	E	T	X	G	P

TRY IT OUT!

Make a chromosome!

WHAT YOU'LL NEED

- Modeling clay

INSTRUCTIONS

1. CREATE A SAUSAGE
Take a ball of modeling clay and roll it into a long sausage shape.
2. PINCH IT!
Make a pinch two thirds of the way up.
3. MAKE ANOTHER ONE
Now, make another sausage shape, exactly the same.
4. MAKE AN X SHAPE
Join the two sausages together at the pinch points to make an X shape.

WHAT HAVE YOU LEARNED?

Your chromosomes aren't always X-shaped. In fact, most of the time they look like just one of those clay sausages. They only become X-shaped just before they're about to divide. Cells copy each chromosome to make a second one exactly the same, just like you did with your clay.

© Getty Images

YOUR DNA

DNA is the molecule of life. It is the reason we are all here today! It's like a code book that carries the instructions to make a human. It stores your genes and passes them to the next generation.

The letters "DNA" stand for deoxyribonucleic acid, which you say like this: de-ock-see-ry-bow-new-clay-ick acid. It's a very long word for a very long molecule!

WHO DISCOVERED DNA?

Friedrich Miescher

This scientist discovered DNA in 1869 by looking at cells on bandages filled with pus!

BACKBONE

I am the outside of the DNA molecule. I look a bit like a ribbon! I am made from sugar molecules and phosphate (pronounced fos-fate) molecules. I hold the DNA bases together in a long string so that the cell can read the instructions in the right order.

LET'S BREAK IT DOWN

If you look at pictures of DNA, you'll see that it looks a bit like a twisted ladder, with two long strings on either side and rungs in the middle. Those rungs are where your body stores the genetic code.

The D in DNA is the molecule that makes up the strings at either side of the DNA ladder. It's a special type of sugar called deoxyribose. The N and A are the molecules that make up the rungs of the ladder. They stand for "nucleic acids," and they are the letters of the genetic code.

BASE

I am the part of the DNA that stores the genetic code. There are four of me: adenine (pronounced a-den-een), guanine (pronounced gwa-neen), cytosine (pronounced sy-toe-seen), and thymine (pronounced thy-meen). Together, we spell out the instructions to make your body!

THERE ARE FOUR TYPES:

adenine (pronounced a-den-een)
guanine (pronounced gwa-neen)
cytosine (pronounced sy-toe-seen) and
thymine (pronounced thy-meen)

BASE PAIRS

The bases in your DNA like to be in pairs. Adenine always pairs with thymine, and cytosine always pairs with guanine. These pairs zip the two halves of the DNA molecule together, and make it wind around in a helix shape.

The letters of the genetic code work a bit like the letters you see on this page. In English, we have twenty-six letters, which we put together to spell different words. DNA has four letters, and they spell words too!

The words in your DNA are the instructions that tell your cells how to make and look after your body. They're written in a code that only your cells can understand. Scientists worked hard to crack that code, and found out that the letters spell out sixty-four three-letter words. Those words tell your cells how to make proteins. Turn to the page about ribosomes to find out more about how that works.

WATCH THIS!

DNA'S UNSUNG HERO

SCAN WITH YOUR PHONE OR TABLET

https://bit.ly/2X9C5oZ

THE STORY OF DNA: HOW IT WAS FOUND

WHAT IS A CELL?
In the 1860s, scientists weren't sure what cells were. Miescher was trying to find out.

COLLECTING BANDAGES
He knew that he could find white blood cells in the pus inside used bandages. Yuck!

LOOK INSIDE THE CELLS
Miescher looked inside the cells, and found a strange new molecule inside the nucleus.

WHAT IS THE MOLECULE?
The molecule contained the elements hydrogen, oxygen, nitrogen, and phosphorus.

GIVE IT A NAME
Miescher called the new molecule "nuclein." Other scientists would later rename it DNA.

COMPLETE THE PUZZLE

Create the picture by placing the pieces in the right squares.

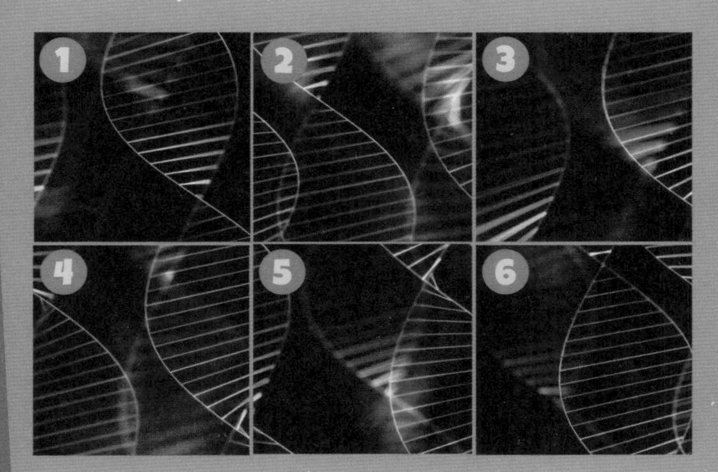

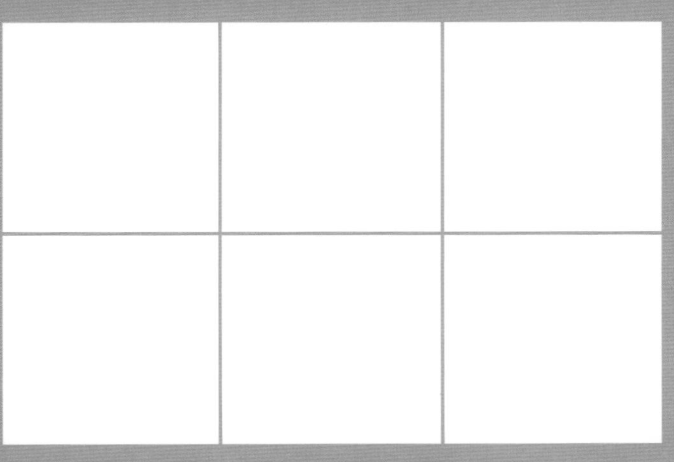

COLOR IT IN!

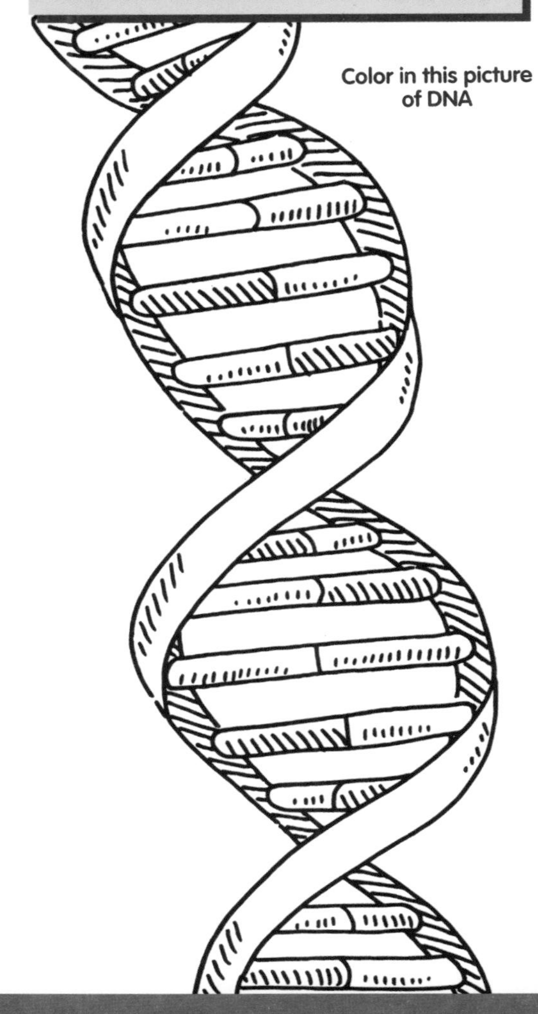

Color in this picture of DNA

© Getty Images

HEREDITY: WHERE YOUR GENES CAME FROM

Have you ever noticed that people in the same family often look alike? Maybe they have the same eye color, the same ear shape, or the same smile. They might even behave in a similar way. That's because they share the same genes.

Genes are the instructions for building and looking after your body, so it makes sense that they help to decide how you look and how you behave. Heredity (pronounced heh-red-it-ee) is the science of how these genes pass from one generation to the next. You might also hear people call it inheritance (pronounced in-heh-rit-ans).

All humans have the same genes because we are all the same species. But each person has tiny differences in their genes that make them unique.

Scientists call different versions of the same gene alleles (pronounced a-lee-ls).

Babies get their alleles from their biological parents. They get one set of chromosomes from their father, and one set from their mother. Each set has one copy of every single human gene, so the baby ends up with two copies of each! It's the mix of these genes that decides what the baby will look like when it grows up.

The two copies of a gene often work together to decide what a baby will look like. But sometimes, one allele decides on its own. Scientists call these alleles "dominant." You can find out what that means in the eye color experiment on this page!

The number of genes you share with your family depends on how closely related you are. Identical twins share all their genes! Brothers and sisters share around fifty percent, grandparents and grandchildren share around twenty-five percent, and cousins share around twelve-and-a-half percent.

WORK OUT THE EYE COLOR

1 EVERYONE HAS TWO EYE COLOR GENES

Each gene can either be brown (represented by a big B) or blue (represented by a small b).

2 THOSE GENES DECIDE WHAT COLOR YOUR EYES ARE

If your genes are BB or Bb, your eyes will be brown. If your genes are bb, your eyes will be blue.

3 BABIES GET ONE EYE COLOR GENE FROM EACH PARENT

What genes they get is completely random. Drawing a box called a Punnett square can help to predict what might happen.

4 DRAW THE SQUARE

Draw a grid with three boxes across the top, and three boxes down the side. There will be nine boxes in total.

TRY IT OUT!

Are fingerprints inherited?

WHAT YOU'LL NEED

- Paper
- An ink pad
- Someone you're related to
- Someone you're not related to

INSTRUCTIONS

1. Write your name on a piece of paper.
2. Press each of your fingers onto your ink pad.
3. Print them onto the paper.
4. Do the same with a family member.
5. And again with someone you're not related to.
6. Look closely at the prints, what do you notice?

WHAT HAVE YOU LEARNED?

There are three main types of fingerprint pattern: whirls, loops, and ridges. You might notice that your patterns are more similar to your relative's patterns than your friend's patterns. This is because you share genes with your relatives, and those genes help to decide what pattern your fingerprints will have.

WATCH THIS!

WHY YOUR FINGERPRINTS ARE UNIQUE

SCAN WITH YOUR PHONE OR TABLET

https://bit.ly/2X44cWD

5 ADD THE PARENTS

Cross out the top left box. Write a big B or a small b in two boxes to the left, and the two boxes below.

6 MAKE THE BABIES

In the other four boxes, write the letter from the box above, and the box to the left.

X	B	b
B	BB	Bb
b	bB	bb

7 WORK OUT THE EYE COLOR

Can you work out what color each baby's eyes will be? Use the guide in step two to help.

QUIZ

Where do we get our DNA from?

DNA holds instructions to make

I have green eyes. What helps to give me them?

ANSWERS: Parents, Protein, Allele

© Getty Images

END OF GENETICS

FUN FACT!
On a genetic level, humans are more than ninety-nine percent identical. Changes in traits account for less than one percent.

So that's how your body knows what to do! Your genes are some of the most important instructions in the universe. Without them, you wouldn't be here. In this chapter, you've learned what they do, where they come from, and how they will pass along to the next generation.

You've cracked your genetic code, and you've learned to read the four letters of your DNA, just like your cells do when they're making proteins. You've found out why your chromosomes are X-shaped, and you've learned the difference between genetic males and genetic females.

Now it's time to go away and explore genes for yourself. Look around and see if you can spot the effects of genetics in your friends and family. Do you notice similarities between brothers and sisters? Aunts and uncles? Grandparents, parents, and their children? If you look closely, you might be able to see some of the traits that have passed from one generation to the next in people's genes.

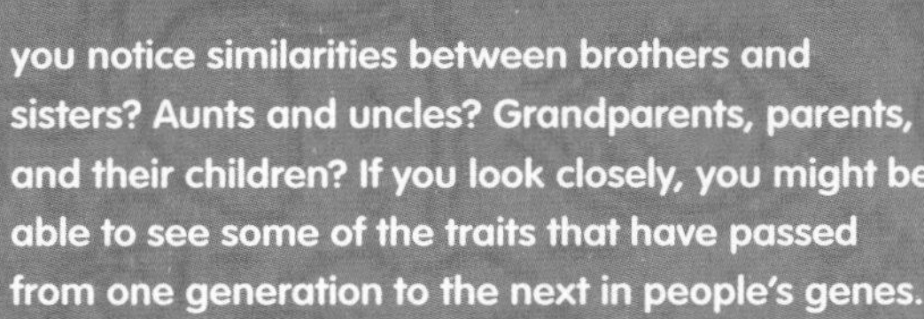

You might notice similarities in animals and plants too. That's because they have DNA just like you.

EASY

22 → X7 → ÷14 → TRIPLE IT → 2/3 OF THIS → +4

INTERMEDIATE

9 → X4 → 5/6 OF THIS → TRIPLE IT → 2/3 OF THIS → ÷1

HARD

62 → TRIPLE IT → 5/6 OF THIS → ÷5 → X11 → +31

FAMILY TREE
Fill in the family tree with the names of your parents, grandparents, and siblings. Who are you most similar too?
GRANDPARENT
GRANDPARENT
GRANDPARENT
GRANDPARENT
PARENT
PARENT
SIBLING
YOU
SIBLING
ANSWER
1/6 OF THIS
X11
-35
DOUBLE IT
=
+56
DOUBLE IT
-24
÷14
=
3/4 OF THIS
-36
÷9
X8
=
© Getty Images

GENE PUZZLES

How much do you know about your genetics?

COMPLETE THE SENTENCES

Fill in the blanks with the supplied words to complete the sentences

1. We get chromosomes from our parents. We get _______ from our mothers and 23 from our _______
2. We share about 98% of our genetic material with _______
3. DNA molecules have a _______ shape
4. Sometimes _______ are inherited through genes

DISEASES

FATHERS

23

DOUBLE HELIX

CHIMPANZEES

ANSWERS: 23, FATHERS, CHIMPANZEES, DOUBLE HELIX, DISEASE

DRAW A TWIN

Russell has the same genes as his twin brother, Ben. Use the space below to draw a picture of his brother and color it in.

WORDSEARCH

Find the words that describe cells in the word search

GENETICS DNA HELIX WATSON
CRICK CHROMOSOMES GENE
MOLECULES INHERITANCE

J	M	G	E	N	E	C	M	C	R	I	C	K	K
K	S	E	K	J	K	O	F	J	O	X	P	M	M
L	D	N	A	N	R	J	I	P	L	H	E	B	K
E	X	E	O	P	W	K	X	S	A	E	D	Y	I
M	L	T	I	Q	H	J	I	E	C	L	O	U	N
O	P	I	P	Z	U	P	H	L	D	I	A	R	H
C	Y	C	N	L	O	I	J	U	H	X	E	A	E
U	P	S	M	G	F	H	X	C	D	P	L	O	R
V	Q	X	S	I	A	H	E	E	E	R	Y	U	I
I	Y	U	X	D	H	H	J	L	F	J	C	K	T
T	C	H	R	O	M	O	S	O	M	E	S	X	A
F	U	F	X	H	X	J	X	M	X	G	A	Y	N
S	I	I	H	J	M	S	K	L	H	I	N	T	C
Q	W	A	T	S	O	N	W	O	J	H	E	S	E

WHAT IS THIS?

Chromosomes can be found in the cells of living things. They tell a cell how to behave. If...

How many chromosomes do each of these living things have?

_______ chromosomes

_______ chromosomes

_______ chromosomes

_______ chromosomes

_______ chromosomes

WORD PLAY

DNA stands for deoxyribonucleic acid. How many words can you create with its letters alone? See if you can pronounce these two words with your friends.

DEOXYRIBONUCLEIC ACID

© Getty Images

ANSWERS: 56, 38, 18, 11, 85

FUN ACTIVITIES TO HELP YOU LEARN ABOUT YOUR BODY!

If you want to find out how your body works, one of the best things you can do is experiment! That's how scientists discover new information. The great thing about the human body is that you have one of your very own to experiment on.

We've packed the next few pages with challenges and exercises designed to help you investigate how your body works. You'll test your reflexes, find your blind spot, hunt for treasure in the dark, and make a working pair of lungs.

You can do some of these experiments with just this book and your own body. But for others, you will need to find different objects from around your house. You might even need to ask a friend, or an adult, to help you.

Before you begin, grab a pen and a piece of paper. All good scientists make notes when they're doing experiments, so you should follow their example!

Read through the instructions for each challenge and make a prediction about what you think might happen before you start. Then, while you're doing the experiment, write down what you discover. At the end, go back and compare your prediction to your real results. Were you right? If not, why not, and what did you learn?

© Getty Images

FIVE ORGAN EXPERIMENTS TO TRY

A LUNG IN A BOTTLE

WHAT YOU'LL NEED

- A plastic bottle
- Two balloons
- An elastic band
- Scissors

INSTRUCTIONS

1. PREPARE YOUR BOTTLE: Using a pair of scissors, cut the bottom off your plastic bottle. An adult can help you with this.
2. ADD THE FIRST BALLOON: Poke one balloon into the top of the bottle. Stretch the opening of this balloon over the bottle rim.
3. PREPARE THE OTHER BALLOON: Tie a knot in the bottom of the other balloon and then cut the top off.
4. ADD THE OTHER BALLOON: Stretch the cut balloon over the bottom of the bottle so that the knot hangs down underneath.
5. SECURE THE SECOND BALLOON: Use your elastic band to fix the second balloon to the bottle. The fit should be nice and tight.
6. MAKE IT BREATHE IN!: Put one hand around the bottom balloon and pull gently on the knot. What happens to the balloon inside the bottle?
7. MAKE IT BREATHE OUT!: Relax the bottom balloon back towards the bottle. What happens to the balloon inside the bottle now?

WHAT'S HAPPENING?

The plastic bottle is like your chest, the balloon inside it is like your lungs, and the balloon at the bottom is like a muscle called the diaphragm. When you breathe in, that muscle moves down, which pulls air into your lungs. When you breathe out, that muscle relaxes, pushing air out again.

TEST YOUR REACTION SPEED

WHAT YOU'LL NEED

- A friend
- A ruler

INSTRUCTIONS

1. SET UP THE RULER: Ask your friend to hold the ruler with the zero-centimeter end pointing towards the floor.
2. GET READY: Put your hand just underneath the ruler, with your finger and thumb slightly apart.
3. SURPRISE DROP: Ask your friend to drop the ruler without warning you. Try to catch it as fast as you can.
4. MEASURE YOUR REACTION TIME: When you catch the ruler, check the position of your fingers. The lower the number, the faster you reacted.
5. TRY AGAIN: Now put the television on, or play some loud music, and try catching the ruler again. What happens to your reaction speed?

WHAT'S HAPPENING?

When your eyes see the ruler falling, they send a message to your brain. Your brain then has to decode that message, and send a message to your hand, telling it to catch the ruler. The time it takes to send those messages is your reaction time. When you're distracted, your reactions slow down.

CAN YOU DIGEST A CRACKER?

WHAT YOU'LL NEED

- A zip seal plastic bag
- A small glass of orange or lemon juice
- A cracker
- An old pair of tights
- A bowl

INSTRUCTIONS

1. SMASH IT UP: Break the cracker into little pieces and tip them all into a plastic bag.
2. CHURN IT AROUND: Add the orange or lemon juice to the plastic bag. Zip it closed and use your hands to mix it all up.
3. PREPARE YOUR INTESTINES: Cut one of the legs off your pair of tights. This will become your intestines.
4. POUR THE FOOD IN: When the crackers and the juice have formed a paste, tip them from the bag into the bottom of the tights.
5. GIVE IT A SQUEEZE: Hold the tights over a bowl and give the mixture inside a good squeeze! What comes out? What's left inside?

WHAT'S HAPPENING?

You're recreating your digestive system! The acid in the juice is like your stomach acid. When you churn it up inside the bag, it breaks the crackers down. The tights are like your intestines. They let your body absorb all the liquid and nutrients in your food, leaving solid waste behind.

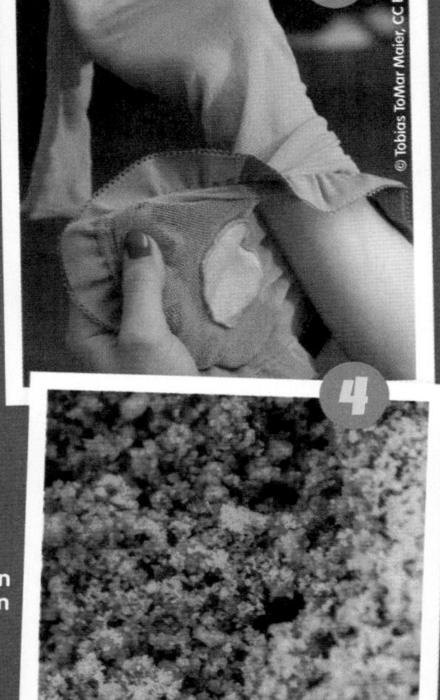

© Tobias ToMar Maier, CC BY-SA 3.0

BEAT YOUR HEARTBEAT

WHAT YOU'LL NEED

- Two buckets
- Five liters of water
- An egg cup
- A timer

INSTRUCTIONS

1. ON YOUR MARKS: Find two buckets, and fill one with five liters of water.
2. GET SET: Grab your egg cup and set your timer to count down for one minute.
3. GO!: Start your timer, and scoop water from one bucket to the other using your egg cup.
4. HOW DID YOU DO?: Measure the water in your bucket. How much did you manage to move before your time ran out?

WHAT'S HAPPENING?

Your heart pumps about an egg cup full of blood with every beat. It sends five liters of blood around your body every single minute! In this experiment, you are trying to race your heartbeat, seeing if you can move fluid just as fast as your heart can.

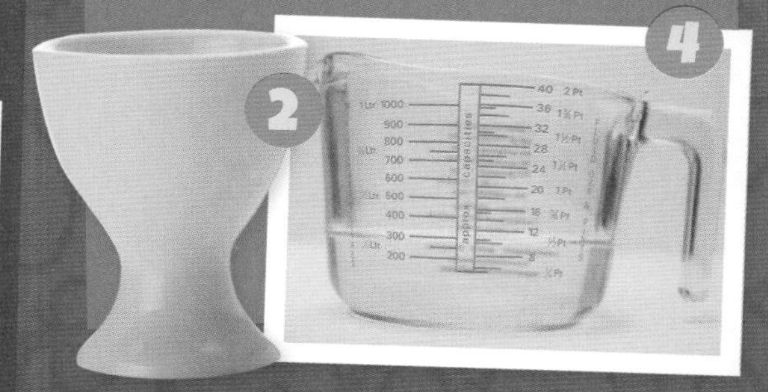

MEASURE YOUR INTESTINES

WHAT YOU'LL NEED

- A garden hose
- A tape measure

INSTRUCTIONS

1. STRETCH THEM OUT: Measure out twenty feet of garden hose. That's how long your intestines are!
2. PICK THEM UP: Wrap up the hose and see if you can get it to fit in front of your tummy.

WHAT'S HAPPENING?

Your dinner has to travel through twenty whole feet of intestines! This long journey gives you time to absorb all the nutrients from your food. This experiment shows you just how incredible it is that such a big organ can fit inside your body!

© Getty Images

FIVE EXPERIMENTS FOR YOUR ARMS AND LEGS

MAKE YOUR ARMS FLOAT

WHAT YOU'LL NEED

- A doorframe

INSTRUCTIONS

1. FIND A DOORFRAME: For this experiment, you will need to stand in an open doorway. Find somewhere quiet.
2. BRACE YOUR ARMS AGAINST THE FRAME: Lift your arms out so that the backs of your hands are touching the sides of the doorframe.
3. IF YOUR ARMS DON'T FIT: If you can't touch both sides at the same time, stand to one side and just use one arm.
4. COUNT TO SIXTY: Push outwards as hard as you can, pressing your arms into the doorframe for a whole minute.
5. STEP OUT OF THE DOOR: Now, step forwards. What happens to your arms?

WHAT'S HAPPENING?

You might find that your arms float upwards all on their own! This is an automatic response. When you contract your muscles on purpose for a long period of time and then stop, your brain takes a while to catch up. It carries on sending messages to your muscles, making them move on their own.

HOW FAST DO YOU BREATHE?

WHAT YOU'LL NEED

- A stopwatch

INSTRUCTIONS

1. SIT QUIETLY: Sit down and relax. Breathe normally and start your timer. How many breaths do you take in one minute?
2. TAKE A WALK: Get up and take a gentle walk around your house or garden, then count your breaths again.
3. RUN AROUND: Now, run around or jump up and down until you start to feel tired. Count your breaths for a third time.

WHAT'S HAPPENING?

You'll notice that the more exercise you do, the faster you breathe. This is because your muscles are working hard. They need oxygen to do their job, and that comes from the air you breathe. The harder your muscles work, the more oxygen you use, and the more breaths you need to take.

THE RING FINGER CHALLENGE

WHAT YOU'LL NEED

- A flat surface

INSTRUCTIONS

1. PREPARE THE CHALLENGE: Find a hard surface like a table, and put your hand down flat with your fingers and thumb out straight.
2. LIFT YOUR FINGERS: Lift each finger one by one. Easy, right? Now it's time for the hard part.
3. BEND YOUR MIDDLE FINGER: Bend your middle finger under so that your knuckle is resting flat on the table.
4. LIFT YOUR FINGERS: Now, take your hand off the table and make a fist. Try opening and closing each finger in turn. What happens?

WHAT'S HAPPENING?

If you find it hard to lift your ring finger off the table, that's completely normal! You'll probably also find it hard to uncurl your ring finger from a closed fist without also moving your middle or little fingers. This is because your ring finger shares muscles, tendons, and nerves with your other fingers.

TEST YOUR TOUCH

WHAT YOU'LL NEED

- Two sharp pencils
- A friend

INSTRUCTIONS

1. CAN YOU FEEL THAT?: Close your eyes and ask your friend to gently touch your arm with one or both pencils.
2. HOW MANY ARE THERE?: Can you tell how many pencils are touching your skin? Try again a few times.
3. TRY DIFFERENT BODY PARTS: Now, repeat the test on your hand, your cheek or your leg. What do you notice?

WHAT'S HAPPENING?

Different parts of your skin have different amounts of nerve endings. This means that you can feel touch better in some places than in others. Your hands and face have more nerve endings than your arms and legs. This can make it easier to tell the difference between one touch and two.

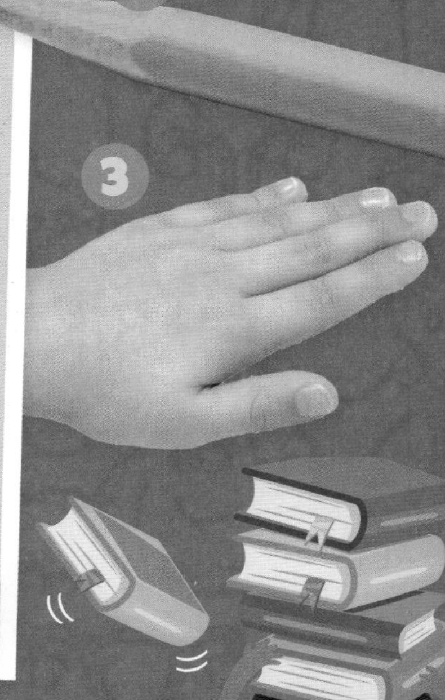

FIND YOUR BALANCE

WHAT YOU'LL NEED

- Somewhere safe to balance
- A friend
- A timer

INSTRUCTIONS

1. FIND SOMEWHERE SAFE TO STAND: You might fall over during this experiment. Stand somewhere safe and ask a friend to stay nearby
2. START BALANCING: Lift one leg up off the floor and ask your friend to start the stopwatch.
3. HOW LONG CAN YOU BALANCE?: Stop the stopwatch as soon as your leg touches the floor again. How long did you balance for?
4. REPEAT THE EXPERIMENT: Try again twice more, and write down the number of seconds you balanced for each time.
5. FIND THE AVERAGE: Add your three times together, and divide by three. This is your average balancing time.
6. CLOSE YOUR EYES: Now, repeat the experiment three more times, but this time close your eyes. How long can you balance for now?

WHAT'S HAPPENING?

If you find it much harder to balance with your eyes closed, don't worry! Your brain needs information from your eyes to work out where you are in space, and to tell your muscles and joints how to move. If you take that information away, it becomes much harder to keep your balance.

© Getty

EXPERIMENTS FOR YOUR NOSE

YUCK OR YUM

WHAT YOU'LL NEED

- A blindfold
- Five smelly things you can eat
- Five smelly things you can't eat

INSTRUCTIONS

1. FIND YOUR SMELLY THINGS: Look around your house and find five smelly foods and five smelly things that are not foods.
2. PUT ON A BLINDFOLD: Cover your eyes and ask someone else to put one of the smelly things under your nose.
3. YUCK OR YUM?: Can you tell from the smell whether the smelly thing is a food or not a food?

WHAT'S HAPPENING?

One of the most important jobs your nose has to do is to keep you safe. There are lots of smelly things around you – some are safe to eat, and others are not. Your nose has evolved to be able to tell the difference, helping to stop you eating something that might make you sick.

WHAT'S THAT SMELL?

WHAT YOU'LL NEED

- Lemon peel
- Orange peel
- Banana peel
- Coffee grounds
- Garlic
- Onion
- Chocolate
- Vinegar
- Toothpaste

INSTRUCTIONS

1. SET UP THE POTS: Ask an adult to put one smelly thing in each pot. Don't peek – your job is to guess what they are.
2. SHUT YOUR EYES AND SNIFF: Choose a pot, close your eyes, and take a big sniff. What do you think is inside?

WHAT'S HAPPENING?

Your nose has 400 different types of smell detectors. But there are way more than 400 different types of smells in the world. The reason you can tell the difference is because most smells contain more than one smell molecule. It's the mix of molecules that makes each smell unique.

BLIND TASTE TEST

WHAT YOU'LL NEED

- A blindfold
- A few different foods, like:
- Apple
- Cheese
- Carrot
- Cucumber
- Pear
- Melon
- Strawberry
- Onion

INSTRUCTIONS

1. PREPARE YOUR CUBES: Cut two cubes of each food. The cubes should measure one inch across.
2. PREPARE YOUR PLATES: Sort the cubes onto two different plates. Each plate needs one cube of each type of food.
3. PUT ON YOUR BLINDFOLD: Cover your eyes so you can't see. You're now going to taste the cubes of food.
4. TRY THE CUBES: Try each cube of food and see if you can work out what it is. How many did you get right?
5. COVER YOUR NOSE: Now, with your blindfold still on, pinch your nose so you can't smell.
6. TRY THE CUBES AGAIN: Try the second plate of cubes. Is it easier or harder to tell what they are now?

WHAT'S HAPPENING?

Most of the flavor of your food isn't in the taste, it's in the smell. When you cover your nose, you're cutting off this vital sense. This makes it much harder to tell what you're eating! Taste can only tell you if a food is sweet, sour, salty, bitter, or umami.

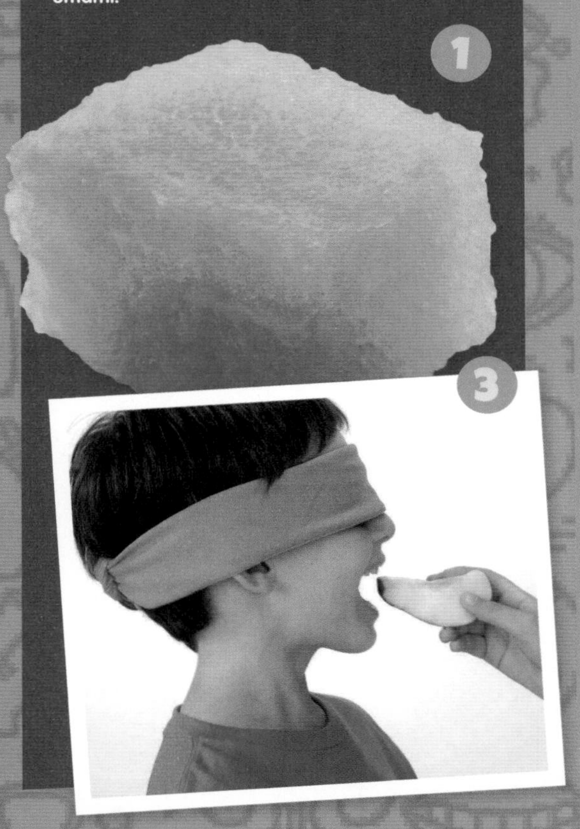

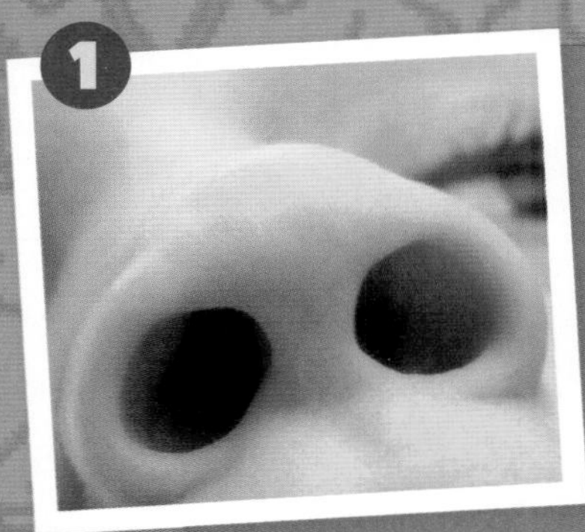

SWAP YOUR NOSTRILS

WHAT YOU'LL NEED

- A comfortable place to lie down

INSTRUCTIONS

1. TEST YOUR BREATHING: Hold your hand under your nose. Does the air come out of both nostrils, or one more than the other?
2. LIE ON YOUR SIDE: If you notice more air coming out of one nostril, lie on your side with that nostril facing down.
3. TRY AGAIN: After about ten minutes, get up and test your nostrils again. Which has more air now?

WHAT'S HAPPENING?

Most people only breathe out of one nostril at a time. The side you're using normally switches every four hours, but you can speed it up by lying on your side. This changes the blood flow inside your nose. The nostril nearest the floor closes and the other nostril opens.

SMELL DETECTIVE

WHAT YOU'LL NEED

- A cloth
- Some perfume

INSTRUCTIONS

1. LAY THE SMELL TRAIL: Spray a cloth with perfume or air freshener, and ask someone else to hide it for you.
2. USE YOUR NOSE: Sniff out the hidden cloth using only your nose to guide you.
3. HIDE IT OUTSIDE THIS TIME: Try the same experiment again, but this time, hide the cloth outside. Is it easier or harder to find?

WHAT'S HAPPENING?

Smells are strongest closest to the source of the smell and get weaker further away. This is because smell molecules spread out and get mixed up with the air. The smell detective experiment is harder outside because wind makes the molecules spread out faster.

© Getty

EXPERIMENTS FOR YOUR EYES

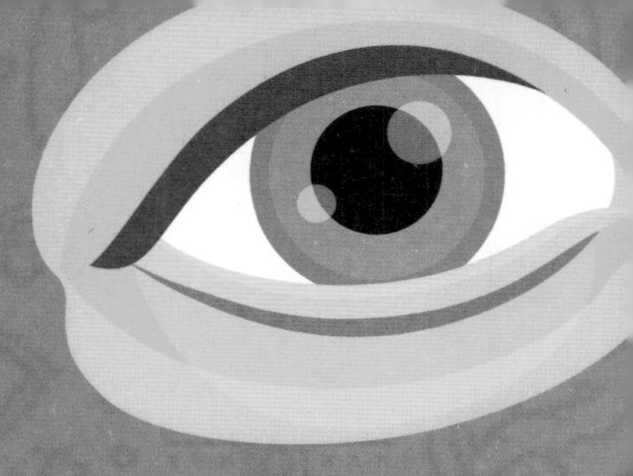

WATCH YOUR WHITE BLOOD CELLS

WHAT YOU'LL NEED

- A bright, sunny day outside

INSTRUCTIONS

1. LOOK UP AT THE SKY: On a bright, sunny day, look up at the blue sky. Be very careful not to look at the sun.
2. DO YOU SEE SPARKS?: Look out for lots of tiny white sparks dancing across your vision – those are your white blood cells!

WHAT'S HAPPENING?

There are blood vessels in front of the light sensors in your eyes. This means that you have to look through your blood to see the world. Red blood cells absorb blue light, but white blood cells don't. So when you look up at the blue sky, these cells show up as bright white sparks.

THE DEPTH TEST

WHAT YOU'LL NEED

- Two pencils
- A friend

INSTRUCTIONS

1. SET UP THE TEST: Ask a friend to hold a pencil an arm's length away from your face, with the non-writing end pointing up.
2. TOUCH THE PENCIL: Take the other pencil in your hand and touch the end of your friend's pencil as fast as you can.
3. CLOSE ONE EYE: Now, close one eye and try again. Is it easier or harder? Did you do it faster or slower?

WHAT'S HAPPENING?

Your eyes see the world as two flat pictures, taken from different angles. Your brain uses the differences between those pictures to work out how far away things are. When you close one eye, it can't do that anymore. This makes it much harder to tell where things are in 3D space.

SEE LIKE A PIRATE

WHAT YOU'LL NEED

- An eye patch or bandana
- A very dark place and a very bright place
- A tray of objects from around your house
- A timer

INSTRUCTIONS

1. CHOOSE THE OBJECTS: Ask a friend to secretly choose a few objects from around your house and put them on a tray. Don't peek!
2. HIDE THE OBJECTS: Now, ask your friend to hide the tray of objects in a very dark place, like under a big blanket.
3. PUT ON YOUR EYE PATCH: Cover one of your eyes with an eye patch or a bandana, making sure no light can get in.
4. GET USED TO BRIGHT LIGHT: Stand outside or look out of a window to get your other eye used to seeing in bright light.
5. GO TO THE DARK PLACE: Quickly go to the dark place and look at the tray. Time how long it takes to identify all the objects.
6. CHANGE THE OBJECTS: Ask your friend to change the objects on the tray while you look out of the window again.
7. TRY AGAIN: Go back to the dark place, and this time, take your eye patch off. How long does it take you now?

WHAT'S HAPPENING?

It takes a while for your eyes to adjust to the dark. That's why pirates wore eye patches. It was bright up on deck, but very dark inside the ship. Wearing a patch keeps one eye used to being in the dark, making it much easier to see.

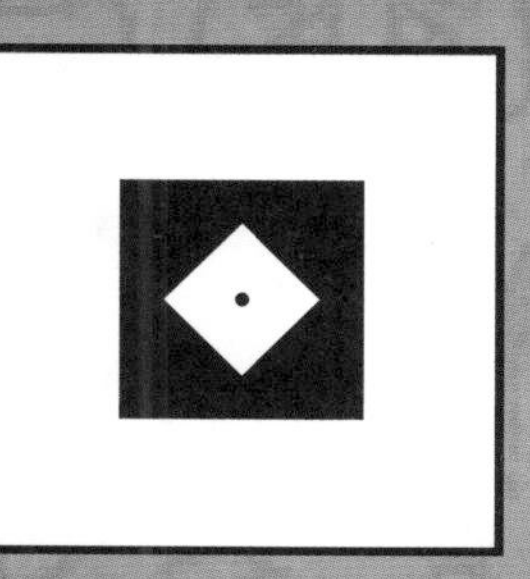

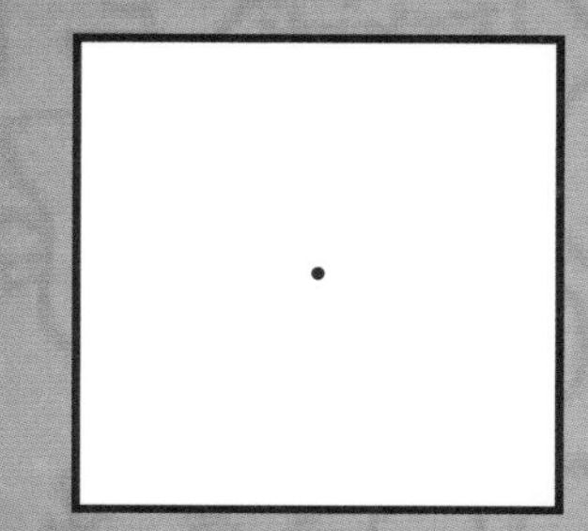

SEE WITH YOUR EYES CLOSED

WHAT YOU'LL NEED

- This picture

INSTRUCTIONS

1. STARE AT THE LEFT IMAGE: Look at the dot in the center of the image on the left. Count slowly up to ten in your head.
2. STARE AT THE RIGHT IMAGE: Now, move your eyes to look at the dot on the right. What can you see?
3. CLOSE YOUR EYES: Try looking at the image on the left again, and then close your eyes. What do you see now?

WHAT'S HAPPENING?

When you look at the same thing for a long time, the light sensors in your eyes get tired and stop working. When this happens, you start to see opposite patterns when you look at a white background or close your eyes. After a few seconds, the light sensors switch on again.

FIND YOUR BLIND SPOT

WHAT YOU'LL NEED

- This picture

INSTRUCTIONS

1. LOOK AT THE IMAGE: Hold this picture about one foot away from your face.
2. FIND YOUR RIGHT BLIND SPOT: Close your left eye and look directly at the dot. Move the page forwards and backwards. What happens to the plus?
3. FIND YOUR LEFT BLIND SPOT: Now, close your right eye and look at the plus. Move the page and watch what happens to the dot.

WHAT'S HAPPENING?

Each of your eyes has a gap in its light sensors called a blind spot. This gap makes space for your nerve cells to carry sight messages to your brain. You don't normally notice your blind spots because both of your eyes work together. They're only obvious when you have one eye closed.

© Getty

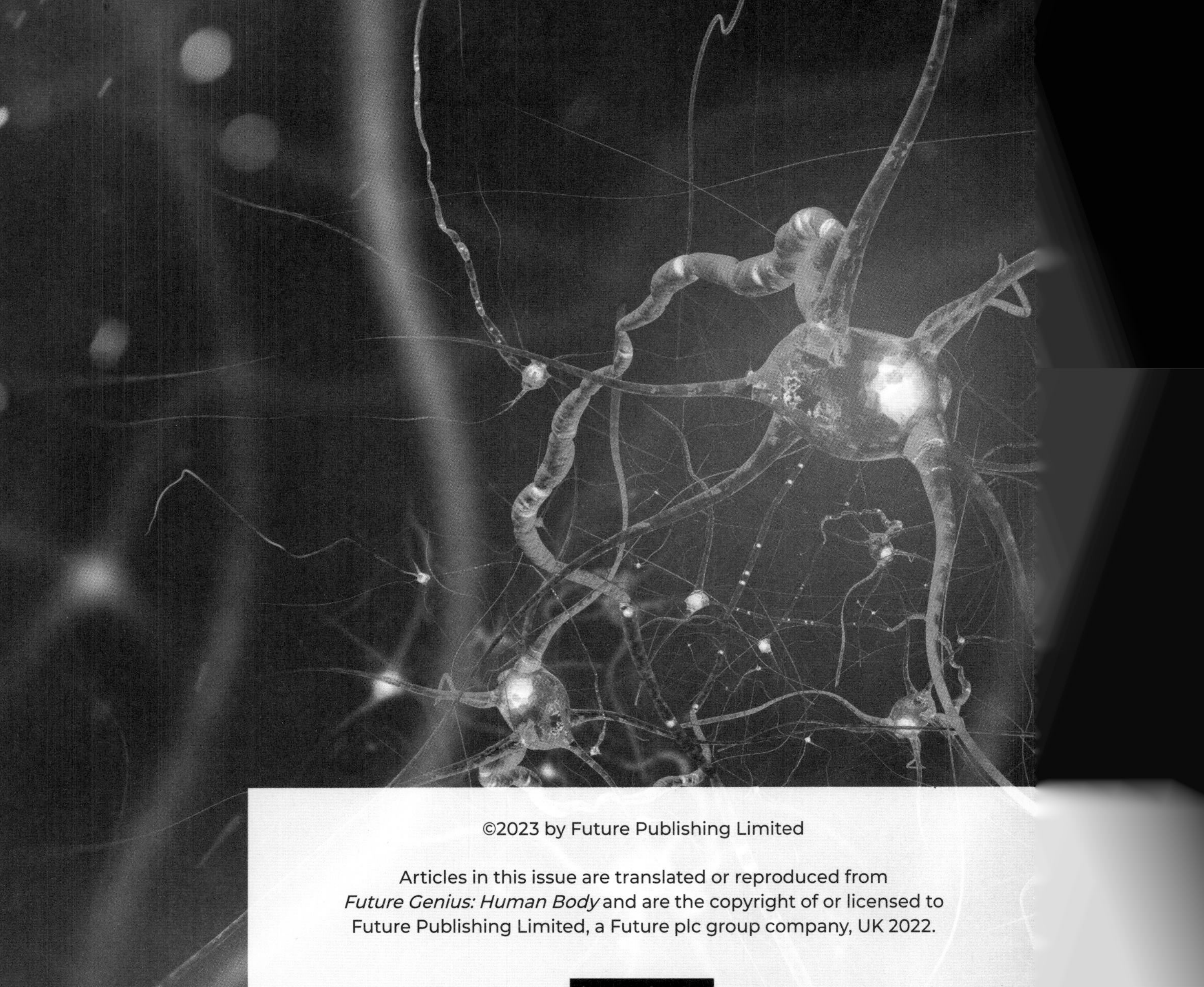

©2023 by Future Publishing Limited

Articles in this issue are translated or reproduced from *Future Genius: Human Body* and are the copyright of or licensed to Future Publishing Limited, a Future plc group company, UK 2022.

Used under license. All rights reserved. This version published by Fox Chapel Publishing Company, Inc., 903 Square Street, Mount Joy, PA 17552.

ISBN 978-1-64124-311-7

Library of Congress Cataloging-in-Publication Data

To learn more about the other great books from Fox Chapel Publishing, or to find a retailer near you, call toll-free 800-457-9112 or visit us at www.FoxChapelPublishing.com.

We are always looking for talented authors. To submit an idea, please send a brief inquiry to acquisitions@foxchapelpublishing.com.

Printed in China
First printing